COURAGE IS CALLING

COURAGE
IS
CALLING

FORTUNE FAVORS THE BRAVE

RYAN HOLIDAY

PORTFOLIO / PENGUIN

PORTFOLIO / PENGUIN
An imprint of Penguin Random House LLC
penguinrandomhouse.com

Most Portfolio books are available at a discount when purchased in quantity for sales
promotions or corporate use. Special editions, which include personalized covers, excerpts,
and corporate imprints, can be created when purchased in large quantities. For more
information, please call (212) 572-2232 or e-mail specialmarkets@penguinrandomhouse.com.
Your local bookstore can also assist with discounted bulk purchases using the Penguin
Random House corporate Business-to-Business program. For assistance in locating a
participating retailer, e-mail B2B@penguinrandomhouse.com.

LIBRARY OF CONGRESS CATALOGING-IN-PUBLICATION DATA
Names: Holiday, Ryan, author.
Title: Courage is calling / Ryan Holiday.
Description: [New York] : Portfolio/Penguin,
an imprint of Penguin Random House LLC, [2021] |
Includes bibliographical references.
Identifiers: LCCN 2021012113 (print) | LCCN 2021012114 (ebook) |
ISBN 9780593191675 (hardcover) | ISBN 9780593191682 (ebook)
Subjects: LCSH: Courage. | Stoics.
Classification: LCC BJ1533.C8 H65 2021 (print) |
LCC BJ1533.C8 (ebook) | DDC 179/.6—dc23
LC record available at https://lccn.loc.gov/2021012113
LC ebook record available at https://lccn.loc.gov/2021012114

Printed in the United States of America
3rd Printing

Book design by Daniel Lagin

Let us not wait for other people to come to us and call upon us to do great deeds. Let us instead be the first to summon the rest to the path of honor. Show yourself to be the bravest of all the captains, with more of a right to leadership than those who are our leaders at present.

XENOPHON

CONTENTS

Part II: COURAGE

Part III: THE HEROIC

The Four Virtues

~

It was long ago now that Hercules came to the crossroads.

At a quiet intersection in the hills of Greece, in the shade of knobby pine trees, the great hero of Greek myth first met his destiny.

Where exactly it was or when, no one knows. We hear of this moment in the stories of Socrates. We can see it captured in the most beautiful art of the Renaissance. We can feel his budding energy, his strapping muscles, and his anguish in the classic Bach cantata. If John Adams had had his way in 1776, Hercules at the crossroads would have been immortalized on the official seal of the newly founded United States.

Because there, before the man's undying fame, before the twelve labors, before he changed the world, Hercules faced a crisis, one as life-changing and real as any of us have ever faced.

Where was he headed? Where was he trying to go? That's the point of the story. Alone, unknown, unsure, Hercules, like so many, did not know.

Where the road diverged lay a beautiful goddess who offered him every temptation he could imagine. Adorned in finery, she promised him a life of ease. She swore he'd never taste want or unhappiness or fear or pain. Follow her, she said, and his every desire would be fulfilled.

On the other path stood a sterner goddess in a pure white robe. She made a quieter call. She promised no rewards except those that came as a result of hard work. It would be a long journey, she said. There would be sacrifice. There would be scary moments. But it was a journey fit for a god. It would make him the person his ancestors meant him to be.

Was this real? Did it really happen?

If it's only a legend, does it matter?

Yes, because this is a story about us.

About our dilemma. About our own crossroads.

For Hercules, the choice was between vice and virtue, the easy way and the hard way, the well-trod path and the road less traveled. We all face this choice.

Hesitating only for a second, Hercules chose the one that made all the difference.

He chose virtue.

"Virtue" can seem old-fashioned. Yet virtue—*arete*—translates to something very simple and very timeless: Excellence. Moral. Physical. Mental.

In the ancient world, virtue was comprised of four key components.

Courage.

Temperance.

Justice.

Wisdom.

The "touchstones of goodness," the philosopher king Marcus Aurelius called them. To millions, they're known as the cardinal virtues, four near-universal ideals adopted by Christianity and most of Western philosophy, but equally valued in Buddhism, Hinduism, and just about every other philosophy you can imagine. They're called "cardinal," C. S. Lewis pointed out, not because they come down from church authorities but because they originate from the Latin *cardo,* or hinge.

It's *pivotal* stuff. It's the stuff that the door to the good life hangs on.

They are also our topic for this book, and for this series.

Four books.* Four virtues.

One aim: to help you choose . . .

Courage, bravery, fortitude, honor, sacrifice . . .

Temperance, self-control, moderation, composure, balance . . .

Justice, fairness, service, fellowship, goodness, kindness . . .

Wisdom, knowledge, education, truth, self-reflection, peace . . .

---

* This is book 1.

These are the key to a life of honor, of glory, of *excellence* in every sense. Character traits that John Steinbeck perfectly described as "pleasant and desirable to [their] owner and makes him perform acts of which he can be proud and with which he can be pleased." But the *he* must be taken to mean all of humankind. There was no feminine version of the word *virtus* in Rome. Virtue wasn't male or female, it just *was*.

It still is. It doesn't matter if you're a man or a woman. It doesn't matter if you're physically strong or painfully shy, a genius or of average intelligence. Virtue is a universal imperative.

The virtues are interrelated and inseparable, yet each is distinct from the others. Doing the right thing almost always takes courage, just as discipline is impossible without the wisdom to know what is worth choosing. What good is courage if not applied to justice? What good is wisdom if it doesn't make us more modest?

North, south, east, west—the four virtues are a kind of compass (there's a reason that the four points on a compass are called the "cardinal directions"). They guide us. They show us where we are and what is true.

Aristotle described virtue as a kind of craft, something to pursue just as one pursues the mastery of any profession or skill. "We become builders by building and we become harpists by playing the harp," he writes. "Similarly, then, we become just by doing just actions, temperate by doing temperate actions, brave by doing brave actions."

Virtue is something we *do*.

It's something we choose.

Not once, for Hercules's crossroads was not a singular event. It's a daily challenge, one we face not once but constantly, repeatedly. Will we be selfish or selfless? Brave or afraid? Strong or weak? Wise or stupid? Will we cultivate a good habit or a bad one? Courage or cowardice? The bliss of ignorance or the challenge of a new idea?

Stay the same . . . or grow?

The easy way or the right way?

Introduction

～

> There is no deed in this life so impossible that you cannot
> do it. Your whole life should be lived as a heroic deed.

LEO TOLSTOY

There is nothing we prize more than courage, yet nothing is in shorter supply.

Is that just how it goes? That things are prized because they are rare?

Possibly.

But courage—the first of the four cardinal virtues—is not a precious stone. It is not a diamond, a product of some billion-year, timeless process. It's not oil, which must be drawn from the earth. These are not finite resources, doled out randomly by fortune or accessible only to some.

No. It is something much simpler. It is renewable. It's there in each of us, everywhere. It's something that we are capable of in a moment's notice. In matters big and small. Physical. Moral.

There are unlimited, even daily opportunities for it, in work, at home, everywhere.

And yet it remains so rare.

Why?

Because we are afraid. Because it's easier not to get involved. Because we have something else we're working on and *now is not a good time.* "I'm not a soldier," we say, as if fighting on the battlefield is the only form of courage the world needs.

We'd rather stick with what's safe. Me? Heroic? That seems egotistical, preposterous. We leave it to someone else, someone more qualified, better trained, with less to lose.

It's understandable, even logical.

But if everyone thinks that way, where does it leave us?

"Must one point out," the writer and Soviet dissident Alexander Solzhenitsyn said, "that from ancient times a decline in courage has been considered the first symptom of the end?"

Conversely, the greatest moments in human history all share one thing—whether it's landing on the moon or civil rights, the final stand at Thermopylae or the art of the Renaissance: The bravery of ordinary men and women. People who did what needed to be done. People who said, "If not me, then who?"

COURAGE IS COURAGE IS *COURAGE*

It's long been held that there are two kinds of courage, physical and moral.

Physical courage is a knight riding into battle. It's a firefighter rushing into a burning building. It's an explorer setting out for the arctic, defying the elements.

Moral courage is a whistleblower taking on powerful interests. It's the truth teller who says what no one else will say. It's the entrepreneur going into business for themselves, against all odds.

The martial courage of the soldier and the mental courage of the scientist.

But it doesn't take a philosopher to see that these are actually the same thing.

There aren't two kinds of courage. There is only one. The kind where you put your ass on the line. In some cases literally, perhaps fatally. In other cases it's figurative, or financial.

Courage is risk.

It is sacrifice . . .

  . . . commitment

  . . . perseverance

  . . . truth

  . . . determination.

When you do the thing others cannot or will not do. When you do the thing that people think you shouldn't or can't do. Otherwise it's not courage. You have to be braving *something* or *someone*.

Still, courage remains something hard to define. We know it when we see it, but it's hard to *say* it. Accordingly, the aim of this book is not definitions. Rarer than a rare gem, courage is something we must hold up to inspect from many angles. By looking at its many parts and cuts, its perfections and its flaws, we can come away with an understanding of the value of the whole. Each of these perspectives gives us a little more insight.

But we do this not to understand virtue in the abstract, of course. Each of us faces our own Herculean crossroads. Perhaps we hold elected office. Perhaps we've witnessed something unethical at work. Maybe we're parents trying to raise good kids in a terrifying, tempting world. Maybe we're a scientist pursuing a controversial or unorthodox idea. Maybe we have a dream for a new business. Maybe we're a foot soldier in the infantry, on the eve of battle. Or an athlete about to push the limits of human performance.

What these situations call for is courage. In real terms. Right now. Will we have it? Will we answer the phone that's ringing?

"To each," Winston Churchill would say, "there comes in their lifetime a special moment when they are figuratively tapped on the shoulder and offered the chance to do a very special thing, unique to them and fitted to their talents. What a tragedy if that moment finds them unprepared or unqualified for that which could have been their finest hour."

It's more accurate to say that life has *many* of these moments, many such taps on the shoulder.

Churchill had to persevere through a difficult childhood with unloving parents. It took courage to ignore the teachers who thought him dumb. To head off as a young war correspondent, then to be taken prisoner and make a harrowing escape. It takes guts to run for public office. It took courage each time he published something as a writer. There was the decision to change political parties. To enlist in World War I. The awful years in the political wilderness when opinion turned against him. Then there was the rise of Hitler, and standing alone against Nazism in his finest hour of finest hours. But there was also the courage to carry on when he was tossed ungratefully out of political life again, in the wilderness again, and the courage to come back once more. The courage to take up painting in old age and put his work out in the world. To stand up against Stalin and the Iron Curtain, and on and on and on . . .

Were there failures of courage along the way too? Mistakes made? Opportunities not taken? Undoubtedly. But let us look to the courageous moments and learn from them rather than focus on another's flaws as a way of excusing our own.

In the lives of all the greats, we find the same themes. There was the pivotal moment of courage, but there were many smaller ones too. Rosa Parks on the bus is courage . . . but so too were her *forty-two years* of life in the South as a black woman without losing hope, without becoming bitter.

Her courage to pursue her legal case against segregation was simply the continuation of the courage it took for her just to join the NAACP in 1943, to work there openly as a secretary, and even more in 1945 when she successfully registered to vote in Alabama.

History is written with blood, sweat, and tears, and it is etched into eternity by the quiet endurance of courageous people.

People who stood up (or sat down) . . .

People who fought . . .

People who risked . . .

People who spoke . . .

People who tried . . .

People who conquered their fears, who acted with courage, and, in some cases, briefly achieved that higher plane of existence—they entered the hall of heroes as peers and equals.

Courage calls each of us differently, at different times, in different forms. But in every case it is, as they say, coming from inside the house.

First, we are called to rise above our fear and cowardice. Next, we are called to bravery, over the elements, over the odds, over our limitations. Finally, we are called to heroism, perhaps for only just a single magnificent moment, when we are called to do something for someone other than ourselves.

Whatever call you're hearing right now, what matters is that you answer. What matters is that you go to it.

In an ugly world, courage is beautiful. It allows beautiful things to exist.

Who says it has to be so rare?

You picked up this book because you know it doesn't.

PART I
FEAR

> Beyond this place of wrath and tears
> Looms but the Horror of the shade,
> And yet the menace of the years
> Finds and shall find me unafraid.

WILLIAM ERNEST HENLEY

What forces prevent courage? What makes something so prized so rare? What keeps us from doing what we can and should do? What is the source of cowardice? Fear. *Phobos.* It's impossible to beat an enemy you do not understand, and fear—in all its forms, from terror to apathy to hatred to playing it small—is the enemy of courage. *We are in a battle against fear.* So we have to study fear, get familiar with it, grapple with its causes and symptoms. This is why the Spartans built temples to fear. To keep it close. To see its power. To ward it off. The brave are not without fear—no human is—rather, it's their ability to rise above it and master it that makes them so remarkable. In fact, it must be said that greatness is impossible without doing this. Of cowards, though, nothing is written. Nothing is remembered. Nothing is admired. Name one good thing that did not require at least a few hard seconds of bravery. So if we wish to be great, we must first learn how to conquer fear, or at least rise above it in the moments that matter.

The Call We Fear . . .

~

Before she knew any better, Florence Nightingale was fearless. There's a little drawing done sometime in her early childhood. An aunt captured Florence walking with her mother and her sister, when she was maybe four years old.

Her older sister clings to her mother's hand. Meanwhile, Florence "independently stumps along by herself," with that wonderful innocent confidence some children have. She didn't need to be safe. She didn't care what anyone else thought. There was so much to see. So much to explore.

But sadly, this independence was not to last.

Maybe somebody told her the world was a dangerous place. Maybe it was the imperceptible but crushing pressure of the times, which said that girls should behave a certain way. Maybe it was the luxury of her privileged existence, which softened her sense of what she was capable of.

Each of us has had some version of this conversation, when an adult does us the cruel injustice—whatever their intentions—of puncturing our little bubble. They think they are preparing us for the future, when really they're just foisting upon us their own fears, their own limitations.

Oh, what this costs us. And what courage it deprives the world.

As it nearly went for Florence Nightingale.

On February 7, 1837, at age sixteen, she was to get what she was later to refer to as the "call."

To what? To where? And how?

All she could feel was that it was a mysterious word from on high which imparted to her the sense that something was expected of her, that she was to be *of service,* to commit to something different than the life of her rich and indolent family, something different than the constraining and underwhelming roles available to women in her time.

"Somewhere inside, we hear a *voice . . . ,*" Pat Tillman would say as he considered leaving professional football to join the Army Rangers. "Our voice leads us in the direction of the person we wish to become, but it is up to us whether or not to follow. More times than not we are pointed in a predictable, straightforward, and seemingly positive direction. However, occasionally we are directed down a different path entirely."

You might think that a brave girl like Florence Nightingale would be primed to listen to that voice, but like so many of us, she had internalized the beliefs of her time, becoming a scared teenager who could not dare to imagine a path other than that of her parents.

"There was a large country house in Derbyshire," Lytton Strachey wrote in his classic *Lives of Eminent Victorians*, "there was another in the New Forest; there were Mayfair rooms for the London season and all its finest parties; there were tours on the Continent with even more than the usual number of Italian operas and of glimpses at the celebrities of Paris. Brought up among such advantages, it was only natural to suppose that Florence would show a proper appreciation of them by doing her duty in that state of life unto which it had pleased God to call her—in other words, by marrying, after a fitting number of dances and dinner-parties, an eligible gentleman, and living happily ever afterwards."

For eight years this call sat there in the recesses of Florence's mind like an elephant in the room, not to be addressed. Meanwhile, she was vaguely aware that all was not right in the Victorian world. Life expectancy was barely forty years at birth. In many cities, mortality was higher for patients treated inside hospitals than outside them. In the Crimean War, where Nightingale would later distinguish herself, just eighteen hundred men out of some hundred thousand troops died of their wounds. More than *sixteen thousand* died of disease, and thirteen thousand more were rendered unable to serve. Even in peacetime, conditions were terrible, and to enlist was itself life-threatening. "You might as well take 1,100 men every year out upon Salisbury Plain and shoot them," she once told officials.

But as urgent as that crisis was—as fast as the altar of murdered men grew—the fear was greater.

There was china to look after, Strachey wrote. Her father expected her to read to him. She needed to find someone to marry. There was gossip to discuss. There was nothing to do, and that was all that a woman of means was allowed to do: *nothing.*

Barraged with this banal pressure, Florence ignored the call, afraid to let it intrude on polite society. Sure, she helped the occasional sick neighbor. She read books. She met interesting people like Dr. Elizabeth Blackwell, the first female doctor. But still, at twenty-five, when she was offered an opportunity to volunteer at the Salisbury Hospital, she let her mother squelch it. Work in a hospital? Why, they'd sooner she become a prostitute!

After eight years of denial, another call came. The voice asked, more pointedly this time: *Are you going to let reputation hold you back from service?* That was precisely the fear: What would people think? Could she break with the family who wished to hold her close to them? To go from a rich debutante to a *nurse*? Could she pursue a vocation she knew next to nothing about—which in the nineteenth century hardly existed? Could she do what women were not supposed to do? Could she succeed at it?

This fear was strong, as it is in every person when they consider uncharted waters, when they consider blowing up their lives to do something new or different. When everyone tells you that you'll fail, that you're wrong, how could you not listen? It's a terrible paradox: You'd have to be crazy not to hear them when they tell you you're crazy.

And what about when they try to guilt you? When they try to punish you? What if you're afraid to let people down? That's what Nightingale faced. Parents who took her ambition as an indictment of their own lack of ambition. Her mother wept that she was planning to "disgrace herself," while her father raged at her for being spoiled and ungrateful.

These were painful lies that she internalized. "Dr. Howe," Florence once ventured to ask Samuel Gridley Howe, physician and husband to Julia Ward Howe, the author of the "Battle Hymn of the Republic," "do you think it would be unsuitable and unbecoming for a young Englishwoman to devote herself to works of charity in hospitals? Do you think it would be a dreadful thing?" Her questions were loaded with so many assumptions. *Unsuitable. Unbecoming. Dreadful.*

She was torn—did she want permission to follow her dream, or permission to leave it unfulfilled? "My dear Miss Florence," Howe answered, "it would be unusual, and in England whatever is unusual is thought to be unsuitable; but I say to you 'go forward,' if you have a vocation for that way of life, act up to your inspiration and you will find there is never anything unbecoming or unladylike in doing your duty for the good of others. Choose, go on with it, wherever it may lead you."

But that fear of being unusual, of more guilt trips, more

threats, remained. All of it was designed to keep her at home, to keep her *within bounds*. And as is so often the case, it worked—despite the explicit encouragement from someone she admired.

"What a murderer am I to disturb their happiness," Florence would write in her diary. "What am I that their life is not good enough for me?" Her family would hardly speak to her, she recounted, "I was treated as if I had come from committing a crime." For *years,* these tactics worked. "She had the capacity to assert herself," her biographer Cecil Woodham-Smith writes, "but she did not. The bonds which bound her were only of straw, but she did not break them."

Nightingale was not the exception in this—in the 1840s or today. Indeed, in the so-called Hero's Journey, the "call to adventure" is followed in almost all cases by what? *The refusal of the call.* Because it's too hard, too scary, because they must obviously have picked the wrong person. That's the conversation Nightingale had with herself, not for a little while but for *sixteen years.*

Fear does this. It keeps us from our destiny. It holds us back. It freezes us. It gives us a million reasons why. Or why not.

"How very little can be done under the spirit of fear," Nightingale would later write. A good chunk of the first three decades of her life had been proof. But she also knew that there had been a brief moment where she had once not been afraid. She needed to seize that power inside herself again, to break out on her own and accept the call she had been given to hear.

It was a terrifying leap. Walking away from a life of ease. Flouting convention. The chorus of doubts and demands. Of course this had held her back—it holds so many of us back. But for Nightingale it would no longer. Two weeks later, she took the leap.

"I must expect no sympathy or help from them," she wrote of her decision to break free. "I must *take* some things, as few as I can, to enable me to live. I must *take* them, they will not be given to me."

Within a year, she was setting up field hospitals for wounded troops in Crimea. The conditions were horrendous. Men died in the halls of buildings and on the decks of ships for lack of beds. Rats stole food from their plates. Patients huddled in freezing rooms without clothes, some spending their last moments on earth completely naked. Their rations were unsuitable, and their doctors incompetent. It was everything her parents had tried to prevent her from sullying herself with. It was enough to scare away even the bravest of public servants.

"I have been well acquainted," she explained, "with the dwellings of the worst parts of most of the great cities in Europe, but have never been in any atmosphere which I could compare with that of the Barrack Hospital at night." By now the fear was gone. In its place was steely determination. She funded the repairs out of her own pocket and got to work.

Henry Wadsworth Longfellow would capture her heroic image perfectly in one of his poems, contrasting the dreary, cheerless corridors of the hospital with the image of Florence Nightingale, going from room to room, carrying a lamp and her good cheer.

> On England's annals, through the long
> Hereafter of her speech and song,
> That light its rays shall cast
> From portals of the past.

> A Lady with a Lamp shall stand
> In the great history of the land,
> A noble type of good,
> Heroic womanhood.

Heroic, *period*. Possible only because she was brave enough to overcome those pedestrian but powerful fears.

Her work in Crimea, done under fire and at grave personal risk—indeed, she picked up "Crimean fever" (brucellosis), which plagued her for the rest of her life—would inspire the founding of the Red Cross. Her innovations, her pioneering work afterward in systematizing the care of the sick and vulnerable, continues to benefit anyone who has ever been to a hospital in the 180 years since she stepped off the path that so many others had tried to intimidate her into staying on.

Her mother had wept when her daughter asserted herself. "We are ducks who have hatched a wild swan," she said. Imagine crying because your child turned out to be special. Imagine growing up in a house where that happened. As Strachey would write, Nightingale's mother was incorrect. Her daughter was not a swan. They had birthed an *eagle*. It had been a long time incubating, a long time in the nest, but once it flew, it was fearless.

What we are to do in this life comes from somewhere beyond us; it's bigger than us. We are each called to be something. We are selected. We are chosen . . . but will we choose to accept this? Or will we run away?

That is our call.

One way to see Nightingale's story is that she spent years ignoring her call to service. The other is that she was preparing herself for the mission of her life. It took time for her to see through the smoke and noise of the family and society that attempted to discourage her from doing what needed to be done. It took time for her to acquire the skills she needed to transform nursing.

In either version, fear—and the triumph over it—is the defining battle of her existence. Just as it has been for anyone who has changed the world. There is nothing worth doing that is not scary. There is no one who has achieved greatness without wrestling with their own doubts, anxieties, limitations, and demons.

As it turns out, for Nightingale this experience was itself formative. When she finally threw herself into the establishment of hospitals and the reformation of Britain's military and civilian health systems, she faced incredible opposition—from bureaucracy, from the elements, from the political powers that be. She had to be more than an angel of mercy in the sick ward: She was a quartermaster, a shadow secretary, a lobbyist, a whistleblower, an activist, and an administrator. It would be her ability to do this, persisting in the face of this relentless and intimidating opposition, to wage a patient but indefatigable battle against those who wanted to deter her, that would make her work possible.

No one could intimidate her any longer. She could not be bullied.

"Your letter is written from Belgrave Square," she said in a letter challenging Britain's secretary of state for war, "I write from a hut in the Crimea. The point of site is different." This from the woman who a few months earlier was afraid to disappoint her hysterical mother. Now when a doctor—or anyone—told her that something could not be done, she replied with quiet authority, "But it must be done." And if it wasn't—for instance, when a hospital she worked at refused to admit Catholics and Jews—she threatened to resign. They got the message.

Her experiences with fear helped her relate to and love the thousands of wounded, dying patients she would care for. "Apprehension, uncertainty, waiting, expectation, fear of surprise, do a patient more harm than any exertion," Nightingale wrote. "Remember he is face to face with his enemy all the time, internally wrestling with him, having long imaginary conversations with him." This was a battle she knew firsthand, one she could help them win.

Today, each of us receives our own call.

To service.

To take a risk.

To challenge the status quo.

To run *toward* while others run away.

To rise above our station.

To do what people say is impossible.

There will be so many reasons why this will feel like the wrong thing to do. There will be incredible pressure to put these thoughts, these dreams, this *need,* out of our mind. Depending on where we are and what we seek to do, the resistance we face may be simple incentives . . . or outright violence.

Fear will make itself felt. It always does.

Will we let it prevent us from answering the call? Will we leave the phone ringing?

Or will we inch ourselves closer and closer, as Nightingale did, steeling ourselves, preparing ourselves, until we're ready to do what we were put here to do?

The Important Thing
Is to Not Be Afraid

~

I t's easy to be scared. Especially lately.

Events can escalate at any moment. There is uncertainty. You could lose your job. Then your house and your car. Something could even happen with your kids.

Of course we're going to feel something when things are shaky like this. How could we not?

Even the ancient Stoics, supposedly the masters of all emotion, conceded that we'll have involuntary reactions. To loud noises. To uncertainty. To being attacked.

They had a word for these immediate, precognitive impressions of things: *phantasiai*. And they were not to be trusted.

Do you know what the most repeated phrase in the Bible is? It's "Be not afraid." Over and over again these words appear, a warning from on high not to let *phantasiai* rule the day.

"Be strong and of good courage," we hear in the book of Joshua, "do not be afraid nor be dismayed." In Deuteronomy, "When thou goest out to battle against thine enemies, and seest horses, and chariots, and a people more than thou, be not afraid of them." In Proverbs, "Be not afraid of sudden fear, neither of the desolation of the wicked, when it cometh." In Deuteronomy, again, echoing the book of Joshua, Moses calls to Joshua and sends him to Israel. "Be strong and courageous," he says to him, "for you must go with this people into the land that the Lord swore to their ancestors to give them, and you must divide it among them as their inheritance . . . Do not be afraid; do not be discouraged."*

The Stoics, the Christians—they didn't fault anyone for having an emotional reaction. They only cared what you did *after the shine of that feeling wore off.*

"Be scared. You can't help that," William Faulkner put it. "But don't be *afraid.*"

It's an essential distinction. A scare is a temporary rush of a feeling. That can be forgiven. Fear is a state of being, and to allow it to rule is a disgrace.

One helps you—makes you alert, wakes you up, informs you of danger. The other drags you down, weakens you, even paralyzes you.

In an uncertain world, in a time of vexing, complicated problems, fear is a liability. Fear holds you back.

It's okay to be scared. Who wouldn't be? It's not okay to let that stop you.

---

* If the Bible doesn't work for you, some version of "Be brave," "Have courage," and "Don't be scared" appears more than a dozen times in the *Odyssey.*

There is a Hebrew prayer that dates back to the early 1800s: כל העולם כולו גשר צר מאוד והעיקר לא לפחד כלל. "The world is a narrow bridge, and the important thing is not to be afraid."

The wisdom of that expression has sustained the Jewish people through incredible adversity and terrible tragedies. It was even turned into a popular song that was broadcast to troops and citizens alike during the Yom Kippur War. It's a reminder: Yes, things are dicey, and it's easy to be scared if you look down instead of forward. Fear will not help.

It never does.

When the markets crashed in October 1929, America faced a horrendous economic crisis that lasted ten years. Banks failed. Investors were wiped out. Unemployment was some 20 percent.

Franklin Delano Roosevelt succeeded a president who had tried and failed for *three and a half years* to make a dent in the problem. Was he scared? Of course he was. How could he not have been? *Everyone* was scared.

But what he counseled in that now legendary inaugural address in 1933 was that *fear* was a choice. Fear was the real enemy. Because it only made the situation worse. It would destroy the remaining banks. It would turn people against one another. It would prevent the implementation of cooperative solutions.

Who does good work when they are afraid? Who can see clearly when they're afraid? Who can help others? How can you love when you're afraid? How can you do *anything* when you're afraid?

The receiver can't catch the football if they flinch in anticipation of the hit. The artist can't deliver the performance if they tremble at the ready pens of the critics. The politician will rarely make the right decision if they worry about the consequences at the polls. The family will never get started if all the couple can think about is how hard it's going to be.

There is no room for fear. Not with what we want to do, anyway.

This life we're living—this world we inhabit—is a scary place. If you peer over the side of a narrow bridge, you can lose the heart to continue. You freeze up. You sit down. You don't make good decisions. You don't see or think clearly.

The important thing is that we are not afraid.

We Defeat Fear with Logic

~

The great Athenian statesman Pericles once came upon his troops and found they had been paralyzed by the portents of a storm. It seems silly, but how would you feel if you lived in a time when people had no idea what thunder was or what caused it?

Pericles could not fully explain the science of what was happening, but he could get close. Grabbing two large rocks, he assembled his men and began to smash the rocks together. *BOOM. BOOM. BOOM.*

What do you think thunder is, he said, but the clouds doing the same thing?

It has been said that leaders are dealers in hope, but in a more practical sense, they are also slayers of fear.

"False Evidence Appearing Real." In sobriety circles, as they work to comfort and assuage the worries that hold an addict back from making changes or trying new things, that's what they call F.E.A.R. False impressions that feel real.

What we need to do is explore our impressions—for ourselves, for others. We must break them down logically, as Pericles did. Go to the root of it. Understand it. Explain it.

In another instance, as the plague ravaged Athens, Pericles embarked with the navy to take the war to the enemy. But suddenly, just as his troops were leaving and he had boarded his ship, an eclipse blocked out the sun. Fear spread rapidly through the men, who regarded this surprise as a dangerous omen. It wasn't with a great speech that Pericles inspired his men to rally, but with a simple bit of logic. He walked up to a steersman and covered him with his cloak. "How," he said, "is what has happened any different except that something larger than my cloak has caused the darkness."

Life is still unpredictable. There is so much we don't know. Of course we're easily alarmed. Of course we're at the whim of our fears and doubts.

The only way through is to attack that fear. Logically. Clearly. Empathetically.

Bravery, Pericles, told his fellow Athenians as the losses from the war and the plague piled up, was the ability to do this. They needed to be calm and rational and clear. We need to break down what's in front of us, he said, learn "the meaning of what is sweet in life and what is terrible, and then go out, undeterred, to meet what is to come."

The part of your brain that sees the worst, that extrapolates out the craziest scenario and consistently underestimates your ability to handle it? This is not your friend. Nor is it the truth. The voice that roots against you? The tendency to catastrophize and exaggerate? This is not helpful. It's not giving you an accurate picture of the world. It's certainly not making you braver!

Tell yourself: It's just money. It's just a bad article. It's just a meeting with people yelling at one another. Is that something you need to be afraid of?

Break it down. Really look at the facts. Investigate.

Only then can we see.

"Not what your enemy sees and hopes that you will," Marcus Aurelius wrote, "but what's *really there*."

This Is the Enemy

~

At the root of most fear is what other people will think of us. It's paralyzing. It's skewing. It distorts the very fabric of our reality—makes us behave in such utterly insane and cowardly ways that it's hard to even describe.

"There are many who dare not kill themselves for fear of what the neighbors will say," Cyril Connolly once joked. We care so much about what other people think, we're afraid of them even when we wouldn't be around to hear it.

The paradox of course is that almost everything new, everything impressive, everything *right*, was done over the loud objections of the status quo. Most of what is beloved now was looked down on at the time of its creation or adoption by people who now pretend that never happened. We often lack the ability or the willingness to see that their objections are just a hump that must be gotten over.

After Frank Serpico blew the whistle on corruption inside the NYPD in 1970, another honest cop congratulated him. But why didn't you stand with me, Serpico asked, why didn't you speak up when I needed help? "What?!" the man replied. "And be an outcast like you?"

Um, yes! Because the alternative was what? To allow your coworkers to extort the very people they were supposed to protect? Allow them to collaborate with the criminals they were supposed to protect people from?

People would rather be complicit in a crime than speak up. People would rather die in a pandemic than be the only one in a mask. People would rather stay in a job they hate than explain why they quit to do something less certain. They'd rather follow a silly trend than dare question it; losing their life savings to a burst bubble is somehow less painful than seeming stupid for sitting on the sidelines while the bubble grew. They'd rather go along with something that will tarnish their legacy than raise their voice ever so slightly and risk standing alone or apart for even ten minutes.

How well we would do to remember the admonishment of Cicero—a man who was laughed at for his nouveau riche origins, for his earnest striving and his love of flowery language— that people have always talked and gossiped and squinted. "Let other people worry over what they will say about you," he said. "They will say it in any case."*

You can't let fear rule. Because there has never been a person

---

*As we'll see, if only this fair-weather politician could have followed his own advice.

who did something that mattered *without* pissing people off. There has never been a change that was not met with doubts. There has never been a movement that was not mocked. There was never a groundbreaking business that wasn't loudly predicted to fail.

And there has never, ever been a time when the average opinion of faceless, unaccountable strangers should be valued above our own considered judgment.

There Are Always More
Before They Are Counted

~

It was early in his military career and Ulysses S. Grant was on a long journey across East Texas. Supplies had begun to run low. One of his men was sick. A horse gave out.

There, in dangerous territory, at the mercy of Indians and outlaws and the elements, needing to cover the seventy miles to Corpus Christi to avoid being declared absent without leave, Grant and another man set out by themselves, rushed and vulnerable, with countless creeks and rivers to cross in hostile territory filled with thick scrub brush and rattlesnakes.

Oh, and wolves—the two men heard "the most unearthly howling of wolves." They couldn't see anything through the tall prairie grass, but there was no doubt the pack was near. Near, mean, and ready, as Grant wrote, to "devour our party, horses and all, at a single meal." He wanted to turn around; in fact, he prayed secretly that his companion would suggest it, wanting nothing more than to get away to safety.

The other officer, a little more weathered and experienced than Grant, smiled and pushed on. "Grant, how many wolves do you think are in that pack?" he asked. Not wanting to seem stupid or a coward, Grant tried to casually underestimate the threat that terrified him. "Oh, about twenty," he said with nonchalance that betrayed his racing heart.

Suddenly, Grant and the officer came upon the source of the sound. There, resting comfortably, with mischievous confidence, were just *two* wolves. So unnerved by a danger with which he was unfamiliar, it had never occurred to him to question the racing of his heart or the extrapolations of his mind.

Four decades later, after a full life in public service and politics, Grant would relate that he often thought of this incident when he heard of a group changing course due to criticism, or when someone was considering giving up because of bad odds or an unseen enemy. The lesson in such situations, he concluded, was this: "There are always more of them before they are counted."

The obstacles, the enemies, the critics—they are not as numerous as you think. It's an illusion they want you to believe.

There was another lesson too: Because what do you think those wolves did when they saw that Grant and his partner just kept coming and didn't turn back in fear? The wolves *ran away*.

In 1861, Grant was a lieutenant colonel in the Union army and sent to move against a Confederate army led by Colonel Thomas Harris in Missouri. Even though Grant had been in battle before, even though he'd learned something from those wolves, he was once again afraid.

The countryside had been cleared as far as twenty-five miles.

There was not a person in sight, like a storm was coming and nobody wanted to be caught out in it.

Once again, Grant's heart beat faster, crawling higher and higher up his chest, he said, until it was fully lodged in his throat. "I would have given anything then to have been back in Illinois," he wrote, "but I had not the moral courage to halt and consider what to do."

At the very moment when he was most scared, when he felt that there was no way on earth that he could possibly bear to attack and fight and subject himself to the din and terror of battle, he reached the top of a hill, expecting to crash into the enemy.

Except the enemy was gone. They had fled, hearing that Grant and his troops were coming for them.

"It occurred to me at once that Harris had been as much afraid of me as I had of him," Grant would write. "This was a view of the question I had never taken before; but it was one I never forgot afterwards. From that event to the close of the war, I never experienced trepidation upon confronting an enemy, though I always felt more or less anxiety. I never forgot that he had as much reason to fear my forces as I had his. This lesson was valuable."

The night is dark and full of terrors. We face many enemies in life.

But you have to understand: They are not nearly as formidable as your mind makes you think.

Whether it's the fear you feel approaching a famous person

at a party, talking to your kids about sex, or asking your boss for a raise, the reality is that both sides are uncomfortable, if not afraid. The trepidation is mutual.

You're overestimating them . . . and they're overestimating you.

You think the job interviewer *wants* to be doing this? That they get off on asking you these questions? No, they are scared of screwing up too. The gruff director your first day on set, the drill sergeant with a fresh batch of green recruits, the front office executive negotiating your contract—their aura of certainty is an illusion. They're just as nervous as anybody else. They're pretending too.

And when you get up close, you'll find the mismatch is hardly as great as you expected.

A little awareness, a little empathy, it doesn't make us soft. It gives us confidence.

Now we see what's really there. Now *everyone else* is more scared than we are.

But What If?

~

What we fear, we do not know.
  Not exactly, anyway.

It looms large but distant in the future. Or it sits in our stomach, twisting and churning, but nonetheless vaguely and without definition.

We fear that something bad might happen. We fear things not working out. We fear the consequences. We fear what people might think.

But *what, where, when, how, who*? That we cannot answer, because we haven't actually looked into it. We haven't actually defined what so worries us. Our fears are not concrete, they are shadows, illusions, refractions that we picked up somewhere or glanced at only briefly.

Well, that has to end. Here. Now.

The entrepreneur and writer Tim Ferriss has spoken of the exercise of "fear setting"—of defining and articulating the nightmares, anxieties, and doubts that hold us back. Indeed, the ancient roots of this practice go back at least to the Stoics.

Seneca wrote about *premeditatio malorum,* the deliberate meditation on the evils that we might encounter.

"Exile, war, torture, shipwreck," Seneca said, "all the terms of the human condition could be on our minds." Not in the form of fear, but in that of familiarity. How likely are they? What might cause them? *How have we prepared ourselves to handle them?* For Seneca, the unexpected blows land most heavily and painfully. So by expecting, by defining, by wrestling with what can happen, we are making it less scary and less dangerous at the same time.

"Suppose the oil fields gave out!?" John D. Rockefeller would say to himself as an exercise to keep himself from getting complacent. And so he built his fortune by acting boldly during the repeated financial panics of the nineteenth century.

Several times a day, Napoleon believed a commander should ask themselves, "What if the enemy were to appear now to my front, or on my right, or on my left?" We can imagine that the point of this exercise was not to make his generals anxious. No, it was to make sure they were prepared.

Yet we're too worried about "tempting fate" or "manifesting bad energy" to practice this kind of diligent leadership. And it is in fact the leader's job to think about the unthinkable. For more than two thousand years, military leaders have had some version of the same maxim: The only inexcusable offense for an officer is to be surprised. To say, *I didn't think that would happen.*

Each of us needs to cultivate the courage to actually look at what we're afraid of. We're afraid to go talk to that pretty stranger across the room. But why? What are the possible outcomes? Being made a laughingstock? Getting rejected? We don't want to speak out, but why? Because we might be criticized? Because in the absolute worst-case scenario, we might have to go look for a new job—but weren't we already thinking about that anyway? Because we could die or be killed? Just as we could every time we get on a plane, every time we cross a street, every time we wake up as a fragile, mortal being?

We need also to cultivate the courage to think about all the things that could happen, the things that are unpleasant to think about, the unusual, the unexpected, the unlikely. It's not just a matter of reducing our anxiety about exaggerated uncertainties, it's also about finding certainty in the unknowns—the risk factors, what goes bump in the night, the plans of the enemy, the things that can and will go wrong.

Nothing human should be foreign to us. Nothing possible should be alien.

Douglas MacArthur summed up all failures of war and life in two words: "Too late." Too late in preparing, too late in grasping the enemy's intentions, too late in securing allies, too late for leaders to be exchanging contact info, too late in rushing to the aid of those in need. Too late in nothing getting specific, in not counting as Grant learned, or in not preparing for the appearance of the enemy as Napoleon said.

A bit depressing? Perhaps. But better to be pessimistic and

prepared than the alternative. It was Aristotle who said that the optimistic are the most vulnerable, because "when the result does not turn out as expected, they run away."

Foresee the worst to perform the best.

When fear is defined, it can be defeated. When downside is articulated, it can be weighed against upside. When the wolves are counted, there are fewer of them. Mountains turn out to be molehills, monsters turn out just to be men.

When our enemies are humanized, they can be better understood. What we thought were incredible costs turn out to be clear calculations—calculations well worth making. The risks, it is revealed, were far outpaced by the rewards. Black swans come into view and can be prepared for. Attacks that we've anticipated can be repulsed. The spectrum of possibilities is reduced, the scope of Murphy's Law is diminished.

Vague fear is sufficient to deter us; the more it is explored, the less power it has over us. Which is why we must attack these faulty premises and root them out like the cancers they are.

We were afraid because we didn't know. We were vulnerable because we didn't know.

But now we do.

And with awareness we can proceed.

Don't Be Deterred by Difficulties

~

Seneca prepared himself for all the possibilities and difficulties of life. But there's no way he thought it would *all* happen to him.

War. Shipwreck. Torture. Exile. All that . . . plus tuberculosis. The loss of a child. Nero's insanity. Slandering critics.

On the one hand, he must have felt this was all unfortunate. On the other, he knew that it was making him the person he was made to be.

"He has won without glory who has won without peril," he wrote. "Mucius was tested by fire, Fabricius by poverty, Rutilius by exile, Regulus by torture, Socrates by poison, Cato by death. One cannot find a great exemplar except in misfortune."

Don't worry about whether things will be hard. *Because they will be.*

Instead, focus on the fact that these things will help you. This is why you needn't fear them.

Our bruises and scars become armor. Our struggles become experience. They make us better. They prepared us for this moment, just as this moment will prepare us for one that lies ahead. They are the flavoring that makes victory taste so sweet.

If it were easy, everyone would do it. If everyone did it, how valuable would it be?

The whole point is that it's hard. The risk is a feature, not a bug.

Nec aspera terrent. Don't be frightened by difficulties.

Be like the athlete, knowing what a hard workout gives you: stronger muscles.

"There is no better than adversity," Malcolm X would say. "Every defeat, every heartbreak, every loss, contains its own seed, its own lesson on how to improve your performance the next time."

How could you possibly trust yourself if you had not been through harder things than this? How could you possibly believe that you *might* be able to survive this if you had not survived other things before?

That's the craziest thing about the gladiators in the Coliseum. Would you believe that many of them were actually volunteers? They wanted to see if they had what it took. We all need adversaries and adversity to exist. "Plenty and peace breed cowards," Shakespeare said. "Hardness ever of hardiness is mother."

It's not bad that this is happening to you. It's good training. Besides, not everyone would even have the strength to see it that way.

This moment is a test. They're called "trying times" for a reason.

It's good that it's happening now, instead of later—because later, you'll be better for having gone through it today. Got it?

You think it'd be better if things were easy. You wish you didn't have to take this risk. If only the leap didn't look so damn dangerous. That's just the fear talking.

It's good that it's hard. It deters the cowards and it intrigues the courageous.

Right?

Focus on What's in Front of You

~

The general Demosthenes woke up to find he was about to be attacked by both sea and land.

It was overwhelming. It was scary. He felt it. His men felt it.

So he did the only thing there was to do. He got busy trying to defend himself from the attack.

Marching his men down to the water, he gave them a speech we could all benefit from when we are facing an enormous, perhaps even impossible problem.

"Soldiers and comrades in this adventure," he said. "I hope that none of you in our present strait will think to show his wit by exactly calculating all the perils that encompass us, but that you will rather hasten to close with the enemy, without staying to count the odds, seeing in this your best chance of safety. In emergencies like ours calculation is out of place; the sooner the danger is faced the better."

It could be said that fear is the one thing we all have in common. We all feel anxiety, worry, doubt, stress. From kids to kings, soldiers to stay-at-home parents, we all feel it sharply in moments big and small.

Does this anxiety help us? Cataloging all the dangers and problems? Letting our fear loom large? No!

"Life itself is far too risky a business as a whole to make each additional particular of danger worth regard," Robert Louis Stevenson wrote. It's better to just get to work. To face what you've got to face sooner rather than later.

"Don't let your reflection on the whole sweep of life crush you," Marcus Aurelius said. "Don't fill your mind with all the bad things that might still happen. Stay focused on the present situation and ask yourself why it's so unbearable and can't be survived."

But who did he say that to?

He said it *to himself.* The most powerful man in the world, lording over an enormous empire, commanding the most fearsome army, was himself anxious and afraid.

Of course he was! A plague. A threat at the border. A palace coup. A difficult child. *Life* happened to him.

It doesn't matter who you are, you've probably got something to be worried about. And is the worry helping us? No. It distracts and obsesses us. It takes us down rabbit holes of doubt and insecurity, through fantasies of extrapolation and doomsday predictions. All cognitive costs taking us away from the actual task at hand.

The poet Wilfred Owen put it beautifully from the trenches in France in 1916:

Happy are these who lose imagination:
They have enough to carry with ammunition.

It's when we imagine everything, when we catastrophize endlessly, that we are miserable and most afraid. When we focus on what we have to carry and do? We are too busy to worry, too busy *working*.

There is plenty for you here right now. That's why the Stoics talked about sticking with "first impressions." Just what you see. What's here. Not everything else that may or may not someday be related to it.

This call you have to make. This check you have to write. This tightrope you need to walk, this throng you need to charge into.

It's enough. Too much, even.

On the Canadian astronaut Chris Hadfield's first spacewalk, his left eye went blind. His right eye teared up and froze too. He was plunged into complete darkness, teetering on the edge of an abyss of even more darkness. He would later say the key to such situations is to remind oneself, "There are six things that I could do right now, all of which will help make things better." And while it is worth remembering that, as he said, "there's no problem so bad that you can't make it worse also." We can't forget that all the energy we spend fearing that we'll make it worse is energy not spent making it better.

Whether it's six things or five—or *sixty-five*—the point is, what's in front of you is what matters. The sooner the better, as Demosthenes said.

So how can you possibly do it well if your mind is elsewhere? If you're concerned about how so-and-so is going to react? If you're already half-preparing yourself for failure? If you've already latched on to all the reasons this is a bad idea?

The answer is simple: You can't.

How do you square this "take no thought for the morrow" with mentally preparing for all that might happen, for all the "what ifs?" Seneca, who inspired Tim Ferriss's fear-setting exercise, said we are doing that for a reason, and that reason is not anxiety.

Apply yourself to thinking through difficulties—hard times can be softened, tight squeezes widened, and heavy loads made lighter for those who can apply the right pressure.

It's a tricky balance, but you got it.

Never Question Another
Man's Courage

~

As James Baldwin reflected on the death of his father, a man whom he loved and hated, it occurred to him that he had only seen the man's outsides. Hidden beneath his failures as a parent was a unique internal struggle that no other person is ever able to fully comprehend. That's why the lines of the preacher at his father's funeral hit him so hard:

> Thou knowest this man's fall; but thou knowest not his wrassling.

It's very easy to judge.

It's very hard to *know*.

To know what another person is going through. To know what their reasons are. What interrelated risks they are trying to manage, who and what they are trying to protect.

There is a story about Nikita Khrushchev after he became premier of the Soviet Union. Onstage, speaking to the Politburo, he denounced the crimes of Stalin's regime. Anonymously, some unnamed member passed a note to the front of the room. "Yes," it said, "but where were you at the time?"

Khrushchev struggled to answer, paused, and then replied, "*I was where you are now.*"

Meaning, in the audience. Anonymous. Doing nothing. Just like everyone else.

We don't know why someone chickened out, why they equivocated, why they couldn't quite get there. It's difficult for people to understand what their salary depends on them not understanding. We are not privy to the full extent of the struggle and the burden under which others have broken. We should try not to fault them, for we can never truly appreciate their experience.

What we know is that we have plenty of areas in our own life where fear is holding us back, blinding us, breaking us.

It's tricky: Sometimes people can be bold and fearless in one part of their life and exhibit extreme (usually moral) cowardice in another. Because people compartmentalize. Because we rationalize.

This battle against fear is a full-time job. None of us have it handled so well that we can afford to spend much time monitoring how others are doing with theirs—then or now. The best we can try to do is learn from our peers, past and present, and apply their lessons to our own life.

If you had lived during slavery, during imperialism, if you had watched the rise of antisemitism in Europe, if you had been born in Soviet Russia or in Mao's China, what would you have done? Would you have been able to go against the tides of your times? Would you have been brave enough to think independently? Would you have been able to resist all the incentives and cultural norms of the moment to manumit your slaves or accept your gay son or support women's rights?

Fear is the swing vote in these answers.

No one can truly understand what it would be like to occupy a different time and place, with different assumptions, assumptions shared by everyone you've ever met and everything you've ever read. But it's also pretty clear: What would you have done back then? As Khrushchev said, you'd be doing the same thing you're doing today.

Don't bother with "What would I do in their shoes?" Ask: "What am I doing *now*?"

In your own life. With your own fears.

People are going to break. You have to understand this. People are going to struggle. As Epictetus, shaped by the empathy cultivated from his thirty years in slavery, would say, until we know someone's reasons, we don't even know that they acted wrongly.

We have no idea how terrified the brave were either. "Only the laundry knew how scared I was," Louis Zamperini said as he reflected on his time as a POW in the Japanese Naoetsu camp. Thankfully, this fear never broke him, not fully anyway, not publicly—but it came close. Judge not, lest ye be judged.

Does that mean nobody should ever be held accountable?

For action or inaction? Of course not. It just means that right now we've got plenty of our own stuff in front of us to focus on. Let us mind our business. Let us put in the work where it matters—not in condemnation or investigations.

The bums in Washington . . . The bureaucrats in Brussels . . . The fools back in corporate. Yeah, they're cowards. But what about you? *What are you doing?*

If we are going to indict anyone for their cowardice, let it be silently, by example.

Waste not a second questioning another man's courage. Put that scrutiny solely on your own.

Agency Is an Effective Truth

~

In 2007, the technology investor Peter Thiel was outed as gay by the website Gawker in a sneering, bullying post that mocked him for his personal life. Since he was a fiercely private man, it should not surprise us that Thiel found the spotlight to be objectionable. Silicon Valley, he believed, was a place whose greatness was rooted in its ability to tolerate weirdos and complicated people. What would a world look like where nobody was given the benefit of the doubt? Where a person's sexual proclivities were put up for public consumption? Where every new idea is mocked before it has a chance?

As he asked these questions to friends over dinner, Thiel was told by pretty much everyone, including very powerful people, that there was nothing that could be done. However unfair, however distasteful, what had happened to him was not illegal and therefore impossible to stop. Besides, Gawker had bluffed and beaten their way out of a hundred lawsuits. They had made their opponents cry and beg for mercy.

There is nothing you can do about it.

You've been told that for the same reason he was told that: It's a nice way to tell someone to drop it.

Because Thiel, like so many others, listened to these pronouncements, they became true. He didn't believe he could do anything, and so for years—even with his brilliance and his fortune as the first outside investor in Facebook—nothing happened. Accepting that he had no agency, no power, became, to borrow one of Thiel's terms, *an effective truth.*

This is how it goes, whether you're a billionaire or an ordinary person, no matter how physically tough or brilliant you are. Fear determines what is or isn't possible. If you think something is too scary, it's too scary for you. If you don't think you have any power . . . you don't. If you aren't the captain of your fate . . . then fate is the captain of you.

We go through life in two ways. We choose between effective truths: that we have the ability to change our situation, or that we are at the mercy of the situations in which we find ourselves. We can rely on luck . . . or cause and effect.

Of course, just because you think you can do something doesn't mean you can. But if you don't believe you can do something, if you're afraid of it, it's very unlikely that you *will* be able to do it. Whether that's walking again or inventing something— if you decide it can't be done, it's not happening. Not by you, anyway.

Xenophon, the great Athenian cavalry commander, once found himself trapped in the middle of Persia, one of ten thousand leaderless Greek troops. As he attempted to rally the men who had begun to despair, who had frozen with fear and frustration, waiting for the next bad event, he explained to them the same dichotomy. He said they could choose between two attitudes, one that said,

"What is going to happen to me?"

And the other that said,

"What action am I going to take?"

A few thousand years later, in the same distant lands, General James Mattis reminded his troops of the same thing: "Never think that you are impotent. Choose how you respond."

"Courage is in shorter supply than genius," Thiel once wrote. In fact, fear, uncertainty, and bad advice muted his genius. For all his money, with all his connections, with all his skill and resources, he believed he was impotent.

And so he was.

As you are, about the hard problems that currently vex and intimidate you.

Such is the power of agency—and our belief in it.

We Are Afraid to Believe

~

The psychologist Viktor Frankl, after surviving the Nazi death camps, spoke of his surprise with the "existential vacuum" that had fallen over Europe and the Western Hemisphere. Good had prevailed over evil, technology had triumphed in the struggle over nature and want, and yet no one was happy and no one had any hope. The world, he said, was spiritually bombed out.

Yet it was because of his experiences in the Holocaust that Frankl was not ready to despair. He posed an urgent question to all future generations: Why did we bother to survive that awful hellscape if none of this has any meaning? What gives you the right to be so damn cynical?

Still, the insidious modern phenomenon remains. People don't think anything matters.

The existential vacuum that began in the twentieth century continues to suck us into its dark maw. Religion, patriotism, industry—each day, collective belief in these pillars of humanity weakens. Just look at what we tell ourselves about history. Do we choose to see ourselves as the latest descendants in a long line of ancestors who have been struggling valiantly and against the odds, toward a better world? Or are we the bastard children of irredeemable racists, pillagers, and monsters? Are we the future of humanity—progress—or are we a plague upon the earth?

Slowly but surely, we stripped ourselves of the things that used to keep us going—that used to call us to something higher. *There is no heaven. The state is evil. People are awful. History is nothing but a chronicle of great crimes.* Then you add onto this the effective belief that the individual can have no impact? That they are at the mercy of forces larger than themselves, that they cannot possibly hope to direct or resist?

The word for this is *nihilism.*

Then we wonder why nobody has any courage. What would be the point?

While sad, this attitude is safe because it's based on "facts." It lowers the stakes. It eliminates judgment, pressure, the idea that we can let ourselves or anyone else down. It gives us the excuse to continue as is, never risking, never trying, never needing to put ourselves in danger.

Scholars remind us that the opposite of *andreia*—the ancient Greek word for "courage"—is not cowardice. It's *melancholia.* Courage is honest commitment to noble ideals. The opposite of courage is not, as some argue, being afraid. It's apathy. It's disenchantment. It's despair. It's throwing up your hands and saying, "What's the point anyway?"

If we don't believe in anything, it becomes very hard to find anything worth believing in. We make our nihilism true, just as we do when we buy the lie that we have no agency; or alternatively, that while we don't control what has happened, we do control how we happen to respond. If you fear that there isn't anything you can do, chances are you will do nothing.

You will also *be* nothing. A protected, self-justifying nothing.

"It's a subject nowadays which is taboo in the way that sexuality was once taboo," the novelist Nicholas Mosley wrote, "which is to talk about life as if it had any meaning."

We want to live in a world of brave people, we want to be brave . . . and we're afraid to talk about it because we might look foolish!

The brave don't despair. They believe. They are not cynical, they care. They think there is stuff worth dying for—that good and evil exist. They know that life has problems but would rather be part of the solution than a bystander.

"Life is real! Life is earnest!" Longfellow writes in his famous psalm.

But to even say that—let alone believe it—requires a kind of courage.

Earnest is not easy. Not as easy as fear and doubt, anyway.

We have to insist there is a point to all this—a point to our lives, a point to our decisions, a point to who we are. What is that point? It's what we *do*. It's the decisions we make. It's the impact we seek.

We believe that despite all the doubters and evidence to the contrary. Because we know we have been called to make it true.

Never Let Them Intimidate You

~

Helvidius Priscus, the Roman senator, was commanded by the emperor Vespasian not to appear in the Senate.

It was a summons a lot of people get. The one to stop asking questions. To quit poking around. To be very careful, lest we find ourselves in the middle of something.

What was Vespasian trying to do? We don't know. Maybe he wanted to ram through some piece of legislation to cover for one of his crimes. Or maybe he just wanted to prevent a headache. He just knew that intimidation deterred everyone else in Rome.

"It is in your power not to allow me to be a member of the senate," Helvidius replied, "but so long as I am, I must go in."

"Fine," Vespasian said with surprise, "but you better not say anything."

"Do not ask my opinion," Helvidius told him, "and I will be silent."

"But I must ask for the Senate's opinion," Vespasian told him, growing angrier.

"And I must say what I think right," was Helvidius's reply.

And so inevitably came the threat of death. "If you don't stop, if you say what I've asked you not to say," Vespasian said with the flip of a wrist, motioning to the Praetorian shock troops standing behind him, "I shall put you to death."

While most of us will never receive such an explicit ultimatum, the dynamic remains the same. They want us to toe the line. To get out of the way. To leave things alone. Or else . . .

Will it work? What will it make us close our eyes to?

It works, sadly, even on the powerful. Helvidius was a member of an elite group, and most of them decided to be cowed. It's true even today. Senators still worry about losing proximity to power. Billionaires avoid controversy so as not to be excluded from Davos or their country club. Once-transgressive artists now pander to their patrons and critics.

Even the all-powerful sometimes find it easier to go along to get along. In Shakespeare's *Julius Caesar,* one of Caesar's men asks him what polite excuse he'd like to send so as not to offend Rome's elites. "Shall Caesar send a lie?" he muses in the third person. "Have I in conquest stretched mine arm so far, to be afraid to tell graybeards the truth?"

We don't want to offend. We don't want trouble.

We don't want to lose our access. Or our power. Or our

pension. Or our privileges. We tell ourselves we can pull off the high-wire act.

So we lie. Or we compromise. Or worse, we cower.

It's fear that does this, that turns us into what Churchill called one of his political opponents: the "Boneless Wonder."

Nobody wants to be pushed out. Nobody wants to be turned on or next in the crosshairs. It was hard to climb to the top of this mountain you're on, and now you're faced with the idea of losing it? Or taking a step back? Isn't our access important? How can we help people if we've pissed off the powers that be? Won't we be in a better position *after* our promotion?

Yes, these things are important, but W. E. B. Du Bois was right when he said it was *preferable to stand tall in a mud puddle than lick boots in the parlor.*

The promoter of Muhammad Ali's first title fight tried to get the young athlete to disavow his Muslim faith on threat of canceling the match. "My religion's more important than fighting," Ali told him. Everything he had ever wanted professionally was on the line—imagine how scary that would be—and still he didn't flinch.

"But what's in it for me?" or "But what will happen to my access if I speak out?" are the wrong questions. Instead, what we must be strong enough to ask is, "But what if everyone acted this way?" "What if everyone put their own interests above everything else?" "What if everyone was afraid?"

What kind of world would that be?

Not a good one. Certainly not a safe one.

Which is why Helvidius fearlessly looked Vespasian in the eye and said, "You will do your part, and I will do mine: It is your part to kill; it is mine to die, but not in fear: yours to banish me; mine to depart without sorrow."

And eventually he was banished; he was kicked out of the parlor, and later executed.

He lost his job. He lost his life. Those two things we fear losing most.

But while he had those things, he actually used them.

All Growth Is a Leap

~

It was three and a half decades later and Benjamin Rush still had imprinted in his mind the feeling of signing the Declaration of Independence. No one in the room ever forgot it.

"Do you recollect the pensive and awful silence," he wrote to John Adams in old age, "which pervaded the house when we were called up, one after another, to the table of the President of Congress, to subscribe what was believed by many at that time to be our own death warrants?"

When you sign your name, you put your ass on the line.

Only in retrospect could they have known that they'd succeed. Only in retrospect would they look prescient and brave and strong. At the time, Rush was just barely out of his twenties. He was hurling himself into the most dangerous experience of his entire life.

But he did it.

In the fable "The Golden Key," the Old Man of the Earth shows a young boy the reality of the world, that there is no progress without risk. Moving an enormous stone from the floor of the cave, he shows the boy a hole that seems to go on forever.

"That is the way," he says.

"But there are no stairs," the boy replies.

"You must throw yourself in," he's told. "There is no other way."

It's scary, but there's no way around it.

Tiger Woods would have loved to be able to keep his old swing as he reinvented his game around a new one, but that's not how it works. It was scary the first time he did it, and the second, the third, and the fourth.

All growth is a leap in the dark. If you're afraid of that, you'll never do anything worthwhile. If you take counsel of your fears, you'll never take that step, make that leap.

The times we could have said something. The bets we should have placed. The people we might have met. The lessons that would have been learned. The battles that were never won.

What if there was certainty, if there was a well-lit, well-defined path? If life were like this, no courage would be required.

It would have been nice if someone could have shown Reed Hastings that the certain future of television and movies was streaming. But they couldn't. He had a sense, of course, that it would be. He also had a multibillion-dollar business delivering DVDs by mail. To capture the upside of the former he had to risk the latter. He had to leap into the insane darkness, braving the analysts and the critics and his own doubts too—as every successful leader and entrepreneur who ever did anything has had to do.

No one can tell you that your plan will succeed. No one can tell you what their answer to your question will be. No one can guarantee you'll make it home alive. They can't even tell you how far down the hole goes.

If they could, if it wasn't scary, everyone would do it. And then it wouldn't need to be done by you, now would it?

The coward waits for the stairs that will never come. They want to know the probabilities. They want time to prepare. They want assurances. They hope for a reprieve. They're willing to give up anything to get these things, including this moment of opportunity that will never, ever come back.

"Rather ten times, die in the surf, heralding the way to a new world," Florence Nightingale reminds us, "than stand idly on the shore."

And find a new world she did. Imagine the needless deaths if she hadn't. Imagine if she had never been brave enough to leap?

You are here for such a brief time. On this planet. In this job. As a young, single person. Whatever. How do you want to spend it? Like a coward?

If fear is to be a driving force in your life, fear what you'll miss. Fear what happens if you don't act. Fear what they'll think of you down the road, for having dared so little. Think of what you're leaving on the table. Think of the terrifying costs of playing small.

The fear you feel is a sign. If courage is never required in your life, you're living a boring life.

Put yourself in a position that demands you *leap*.

Don't Fear Decisions

~

Dean Acheson was present, he said with a twinkle, at the creation. Or rather the *re*-creation, when a new world order was built from the wreckage of World War II. He was undersecretary of state under George Marshall, then the secretary of state for Harry Truman. In his retirement, he advised John F. Kennedy and Lyndon Johnson.

There he had a ringside seat to some of the most critical and tense moments in American history. The Marshall Plan. The Berlin Airlift. The Cuban Missile Crisis. The war in Vietnam. The kind of high-pressure situations where the weak wilt and the strong shine, where all that separates the world from chaos and destruction is the courage of good leadership. Where cowardice is not just potentially embarrassing but threatens the lives of millions.

"At the top," Acheson would observe, "there are no easy choices. All are between evils, the consequences of which are hard to judge."

But this is what scares us. Making the wrong decision. Screwing things up. The potential unintended consequences.

What about this?

What about that?

If I get it wrong? If people disagree? If something else happens?

Should you stay?

Go?

Should you say something? Should you try it this way or that way?

But what if it doesn't work?

So many choices. Few of them easy. None of them clear. Scary choices, torturing you, as Shakespeare said, "like a phantasma, or a hideous dream."

We tell ourselves we're thinking, that we're weighing our options, that we're making progress.

In truth, we are paralyzed with fear. Overwhelmed by options. By second guesses. By that hatred of making mistakes. So what we're really doing is making ourselves miserable.

We tell ourselves it's about options . . . really it's paralysis by analysis.

All the while, somebody or someone else *is* making progress.

There is a story about a Spartan king who was marching across Greece. As he entered each new country, he sent envoys to ask whether he should be prepared to treat them as friends or enemies.

Most of the nations decided quickly, and most of them chose

friendship. But one king wanted to think about his options, because he was afraid of committing. So he thought and he thought and he thought . . . until it was chosen for him.

"Let him consider it, then," the frustrated Spartan general said as he fixed his jaw, "while we just march on."

As the song goes, even if you choose not to decide—even if you put things off—you *still have made a choice*. You are voting for the status quo. You are voting to let *them* decide. You are voting to give up your own agency.

"What cowardice fears most of all," Søren Kierkegaard said, "is the making of a resolution, for a resolution instantly dissipates the mist."

What you fear is consequences. So you keep deliberating, hoping you can put them off.

Can't lose if you don't choose? Of course you can. You lose the moment. You lose the momentum. You lose your ability to look yourself in the mirror.

You Can't Put Your Safety First

~

As Julius Caesar sought to overthrow the Roman Republic, because its institutions were getting in his way, Cicero, his longtime rival, seemed to think chiefly of himself. In life and war, Cicero would later say, "one should choose the stronger side and reckon the safe course the better."

Instead of fighting to preserve the nation that he had long served, he just waited to see how things sorted themselves out. When Caesar won, Cicero was there to praise him, even censoring his eulogy for his fallen friends so as not to offend the new dictator. When Caesar was assassinated and Rome was plunged once again into civil war, Cicero put his finger to the wind rather than do what was right.

You might think that this at least had the effect of keeping Cicero alive, but that's the irony. He would soon be killed by Mark Antony anyway. And even if he had survived? His career would have been over anyway because he'd lost all credibility. He died pathetically, losing not only his life but multiple chances to have been a hero.

Sure, it's possible to stand back and let things get sorted out. We can wait to pick a side or a winner. Maybe it'll pay off. Maybe history will leave us blameless.

Maybe.

But deep down, you will know. The fear leaves a stain.

"Never yet," Theodore Roosevelt reminds us, "was worthy adventure worthily carried through by the man who put his personal safety first."

There are things worse than dying. Living with what we had to do to keep living, for one. Regretting that lost opportunity to have been a hero. The hellish existence of a world run by cowards.

Called before a white judge to answer for a controversial sermon, the pastor and civil rights pioneer Vernon Johns could have apologized. He could have folded. He could have protected himself and promised never to criticize segregation or racism. This was the safe thing to do . . . and by the Ciceronian logic, probably the right decision. Instead, he looked the judge in the eye and said, "Everywhere I go in the South the negro is forced to choose between his hide and his soul. Mostly, he chooses his hide. I'm going to tell him that his hide is not worth it."

Fear speaks the powerful logic of self-interest. It is also an inveterate liar.

This self-preservation it promises, the comfort it claims it will protect. Is it even real? How safe are you, *really*?

We are fragile creatures. Nothing can change that. You're a

fool if you think staying on the good side of bad people is a safe bet. The future you seem to be willing to defer anything to ensure? *Nothing can guarantee it.* This moment, the present you're neglecting—whether it's an opportunity to do something risky and fun, or the call to do something harrowing but right—is all you have.

We like to think we can have an extraordinary life by making ordinary decisions, but it's not true. It's actually all the ordinary decisions—the safe ones, recommended by every expert, criticized by no one—that make us incredibly vulnerable in times of chaos and crisis.

It's worth remembering that most people die in bed. Getting up and getting active is much safer!

It is risky to try to make the future in business, the strategist Peter Drucker has written, but it's riskier still not to even try. Because eventually it will happen—someone will try, and then you'll be on the wrong side of the outcome, or at the very least behind the curve. And that's when you'll lose the initiative.

Life is risky. As the poet Dylan Thomas said, each day is "always touch-and-go." No amount of corporate ass-covering will ever change that. No amount of hiding will actually protect you from scary things. We are already fugitives from the law of averages, we are already marked for death from birth. When you realize this, you can stop being so precious, so concerned about every danger and every possible thing that can go wrong.

Who cares? It's just a drop in the bucket, another point on

the risk assessment that is already off the charts as a mortal being.

All certainty is uncertain. You're not safe. You never will be. No one is. In putting safety above everything, we actually put ourselves in danger. Of being forgotten. Of never coming close. Of being complicit.

How will you handle the danger?

"What will happen to me?" No one can tell you that. But with courage, you can say yourself, "I'm not sure, but I will get through it with my soul intact. I will make the best of it. I will *not* be afraid."

Fear Is Showing You Something

~

Theodore Roosevelt hesitated before he invited Booker T. Washington to the White House for dinner in 1901. It was the first time in American history that a black man had ever dined as a sitting president's guest.

He hesitated because he was scared. Scared what his southern relatives might think, for fear of what the newspapers would say, fear that racist voters would abandon him, that he would lose support in the South, that it could cost him the election. A sitting president—the man who led the Rough Riders on a suicidal charge, who hunted bears, who had conquered a crippling childhood illness, who had beaten depression and grief and a million other obstacles—was scared *of what people might think.*

It was a scary situation. As the front-page headline of the *New York Times* would read the next day: "Washington People, as a Rule, Condemn President's Violation of Precedent—Maryland Campaign Affected."

Condemned *as a rule*!

Yet in the end, the fear was precisely why Roosevelt decided to go through with it.

"The very fact that I felt a moment's qualm on inviting him because of his color made me ashamed of myself," Roosevelt said in a letter to a civil rights adviser, "and made me hasten to send the invitation. As things turned out, I am very glad that I asked him, for the clamor aroused by the act makes me feel as if the act was necessary."

No rule is perfect, but this one works: Our fears point us, like a self-indicting arrow, in the direction of the right thing to do. One part of us knows what we ought to do, but the other part reminds us of the inevitable consequences. Fear alerts us to danger, but also to opportunity. If it wasn't scary, everyone would do it. If it was easy, there wouldn't be any growth in it. That tinge of self-preservation is the pinging of the metal detector going off. We may have found something.

Will we ignore it? Or will we dig?

Fear votes for hesitation, it always has a reason for not *doing* and so it rarely does anything. If we don't find ourselves experiencing this hesitation every so often, we should know that we are not pushing ourselves enough.

Imagine, too, though, the hesitation of Booker T. Washington. He was risking his *life* to accept Roosevelt's invitation. He was risking the precarious support of his white southern donors. He was kicking a violent hornet's nest. *We'll have to kill a thousand niggers,* the senator Benjamin Tillman said in response, *to teach them their place again.**

And yet Washington went. Undaunted. Unintimidated. Roosevelt's niece, Eleanor, later talked about *doing the thing you cannot do.* It is almost always the thing you should do. When something tells you that you're not allowed. When someone tells you that you'll regret your decision. When the pit in your stomach makes you hesitate.

But what will our customers think? But what if our competitors use this against us? What if it doesn't work? Will people be mad at me?

Damn them all.

Decide to testify. Decide to go all in on the new venture. Take the creative risk. Decide to answer the reporter's email. Decide to say what you're hesitant to say.

They say not to take counsel of your fears, but perhaps that's exactly what we should do.

We should listen closely and then do the opposite.

---

* Inexcusably, as of 2021, a statue of Senator Tillman remains standing on the grounds of the South Carolina statehouse.

The Scariest Thing
To Be Is Yourself

~

Frank Serpico was the odd man out in the NYPD in the 1960s. He was Italian when most of the cops were Irish. He grew his hair long. He liked opera and ballet. He lived in the Village, while most of his coworkers resided in quiet suburbs. He had a big white sheepdog and wore vests and leather and all sorts of other strange clothes.

And that was when he *wasn't* in costume. It was not atypical for Serpico to show up to work in elaborate, homemade disguises to help him catch criminals on the street—even though he was passed over time and time again for promotion to undercover detective.

He was the odd man out.

Thank God.

A prosecutor working with Serpico complained that the man was difficult. Serpico reminded him that if he had been a little less difficult, and a little more inclined to be like everyone else in the department, *they wouldn't have a case against corruption at all.*

By definition, each of us is original. Our DNA has never existed before on this planet. No one has ever had our unique set of experiences. Yet what do we do with this heritage? We push it away. We choose *not* to be ourselves. We choose to go along, to not raise any eyebrows.

It's incredible to think that in the NYPD, cops found it easier to take bribes than to be clean, but it's true. To stand up would be to stand out. It was to make yourself a target. It was to be different and thus alone.

Out of fear, we conform. Out of fear, we don't do what's right. We mute ourselves. We don't even want other people to be themselves, because it makes us uncomfortable.

Difficult. Odd. Loose cannon. Troublemaker. Gay? A freak? These are the kinds of words that litter the dossiers collected by J. Edgar Hoover or the KGB or the Gestapo. This is what cowards like to call the brave who challenge them. Or pose an existential threat to their illegitimate regimes or injustices.

We mutter those epithets ourselves when we are shamed by the freedom of the people who have the confidence to be themselves.

It's a tricky balance we expect people to figure out. We want everyone to be on the same team. We want them to buy into the culture. In the military, they're expected to dress the same and even get the same haircut. We want people to do what they're told, to follow instructions . . .

Then we somehow expect free thought to flourish, new inventions and ideas to drop from the sky, and people to exhibit extraordinary acts of sacrifice and courage. As if it's possible for these things to exist in a world of conformity.

The pressure wants to smooth down the edges, lessen the resistance . . . or else. *Or else what?* we have to ask. "Though an army besiege me," Psalm 27 reads, "my heart will not fear; though war break out against me, even then will I be confident."

It doesn't matter who or how many come at you, *you have to be you.*

Confidently. Authentically. Bravely.

It's ironic that a pioneering feminist like Florence Nightingale criticized women who tried to "be like men." Just be yourself, she was saying—we don't need anyone apishly imitating anyone else or instinctually rejecting anyone either. We all face other people's expectations and stereotypes. We resist this, and at the same time, we can remember Seneca's advice: We don't need to buck the crowd on every single little thing. We don't need to be different for the sake of being different—petulant rebellion can be its own kind of defense mechanism. But if we do, on the outside, look the same as everyone else, we better make damn sure that on the inside everything is different. That we are truly who we want to be, how we know deep down it feels right to be.

Because the courage to be different is the courage to think different, to see what others don't see, to hear what others don't hear. It's not a coincidence that so many whistleblowers and art-ists were weirdos. It was precisely their weirdness that allowed them to see what everyone else was unable to see.

Be a cop. Be a soldier. Be a philosopher. Be another musician in a long tradition of rock music. Hold somebody's hand. Just make sure that underneath, you are *being yourself*. That you are not letting fear shut you up or put you down. That you are not doing what everyone else is doing simply *because they are doing it*.

Be original. Be yourself. To be anything else is to be a coward.

Don't let the opinion of cowards influence what you think or do. The future depends on it.

Life Happens in Public.
Get Used to It.

~

Jerry Weintraub wanted to be an actor.

He made it into the Neighborhood Playhouse. He studied under Sandy Meisner. One of his classmates was James Caan. There's a reason you've seen movies with James Caan and none with Jerry Weintraub, and that reason is fear.

Or rather, fear by its other identity: Shame.

Sent to get clothes for a dance class—taught by Martha Graham, no less—Jerry and James went to a store on Broadway. As he tried on tights, Jerry, a tough kid from the Bronx, took one look in the mirror and knew there was no way he'd ever let himself be seen this way in public. James Caan, who came from the same neighborhood, whose father had been a butcher, who had the same view of himself as a tough guy, looked in the same mirror. He did not let self-consciousness win.

As the author Rich Cohen writes, "This was the dividing line, the moment of truth. Jimmy Caan put on the slippers and tights, so his name appears in the credits as, say, Sonny Corleone in *The Godfather*. Jerry Weintraub, because he was filled with normal, decent human shame, did not put on the slippers and tights, so his name appears in movie credits as producer."

One would be nominated for Academy Awards, the other would package *The Karate Kid*. Both would be successful, but only one realized that shared early dream—only one was able to stand boldly, bravely in front of the camera, and own it.

While most of us will not make our living on the screen, we all have to face this reluctance to be *seen*. Our fear of what other people think, of embarrassment or awkwardness, is not the same fear that holds a man back from running into battle, but it is a limitation, a deficiency of courage that deprives us of our destiny all the same.

There is no change, no attempt, no reach that does not look strange to someone. There's almost no accomplishment that is possible without calling some attention on yourself. To gamble on yourself is to risk failure. To do it in public is to risk humiliation.

Anyone who tries to leave their comfort zone has to know that.

Yet we'd almost rather die than be uncomfortable.

The comedian Jerry Seinfeld once noted that people rank public speaking as worse than the fear of death, which means, quite insanely, that at a funeral the average person would rather be in the casket than delivering the eulogy.

In ancient Rome, there was perhaps no better orator than Crassus, famed for his brilliant speeches and prosecutions of the corrupt and the evil. At least that's how he appeared to his audiences. You would not have known, as he later admitted, that at the outset of every speech he would "Feel a tremor through my whole thoughts, as it were, and limbs." Even as a master, he still experienced doubt—still felt waves of overwhelming anxiety and fear crash over him before he went onstage.

At the beginning of his career, it was even worse. He recounts his eternal debt and gratitude to a judge who, at one of Crassus's first public appearances, could tell how "absolutely disheartened and incapacitated with fear" the boy was, and adjourned the hearing until a later date. We can imagine those merciful words from the judge, sparing Crassus as he no doubt prayed he would be spared, as we have prayed a thousand times, second only to his hope that he might be struck down and killed rather than have to go on.

Yet we would not be talking about Crassus had he not pushed through that fear.

Would he have rather practiced law from the privacy of his study? Sure, just as Serpico probably wished he could've dressed as he liked without comment. Such is life. It doesn't care about our *rathers*. You will have to stand alone from time to time. If you can't even do that to deliver a *talk*, how will you possibly have the courage to do it when it counts?

You put on the tights. You push through the stage fright— the fright that persists even after you've mastered the art of public speaking. You enter the witness stand. You deliver the hard news to the assembled employees. You just learn to stop thinking about *what they think*. You'll never do original work if you can't. You have to be willing not only to step away from the herd but get up in front of them and say what you truly think or feel. It's called "public life" for a reason.

We don't get to succeed privately.

It's ironic, the Stoics would say, that for all our selfish cares about ourselves, we seem to value other people's opinions about us more than our own. The freed slave Epictetus says, "If you wish to improve, be content to appear clueless or stupid." Can you do that? You'll have to.

When we flee in the direction of comfort, of raising no eyebrows, of standing in the back of the room instead of the front, what we are fleeing is opportunity. When we defer to fear, when we let it decide what we will and won't do, we miss so much. Not just success, but actualization.

Who might we be if we didn't care about blushing? What could we accomplish if we didn't mind the spotlight? If we were tough enough to put on the tights? If we were willing not only to fail but to do so in front of others?

Which Tradition Will You Choose?

I magine the sheer terror of existence for early man. Imagine what it was like to bring a child into a world with a survival rate of less than 50 percent. Imagine what it was like to be at the whim of kings as well as the elements, to have lived through depressions and disasters, wars, and the worries of an uncertain existence.

And what did they do with all of this?

They kept going. They did it anyway.

People who walked over land bridges to new continents, who rebuilt after fires, who cinched on armor and ran into battle, who demanded inalienable rights from their governments, who stared down mobs, who stole away from slavery or lack of opportunity in the dead of night, who explored the frontiers of science—those people, eventually, indirectly and directly created you. Their blood surges through your veins. Their DNA is infused in yours.

Even if you don't come from a famous family. Even if you come from a persecuted minority, you come from fighters and survivors. "You come from sturdy peasant stock," James Baldwin explained to his nephew, "men who picked cotton and dammed rivers and built railroads and in the teeth of the most terrifying odds achieved an unassailable and monumental dignity."

Did he also come from people who had been afraid? Of course. We all do. But we choose whose tradition we are going to follow.

"I shall remind you of the dangers which our fathers have also been through," Xenophon told his fearful men, stuck there in Persia, "so that you realize that it is right for you to be brave and that with the help of the gods, the brave find safety even from the worst difficulties."

We must remember that history is not filled with fairy tales, but flesh and blood. Real people, people like you—people no better, certainly no healthier than you—squared up against fate, took her punches, threw their best shot. They failed, they made mistakes, they were knocked down, but they survived. They survived long enough to put in motion the events that carry us forward today. In some cases, they are quite literally our parents, in other cases only figuratively so.

There were cowards too, but we can write them out of the family tree.

When we are afraid, we can look up at those who came before us. We can visit the monuments they erected. We can read the documents they wrote. Because this is our tradition.

They have passed us a baton. Will we accept it?

"When I am no longer even a memory, just a name," you can hear an elderly Florence Nightingale saying, recorded on a wax tablet at the end of her life, "I hope that my voice may perpetuate the great work of my life."

You Can't Be Afraid to Ask

~

Frontline responders know that their duty is to rush toward the bang while others run away. A parent knows that they put their own interests and needs behind those of their children. The unfailingly cheerful know how much other people look to them for humor and hope.

But do these people know that they can ask for help too?

Do you know that?

Or are you afraid?

Historically, the Stoics were strong. And brave. And did their duty—without complaint, without hesitation. With courage, they carried the load, and willingly did so for others when it was necessary. But it's a mistake to assume that they were somehow superhuman, that they never struggled, never wavered, never needed for anything. They had to—as we all do—ask for help when they needed it.

And they were not afraid to do it, either. Because sometimes that's the strongest and bravest thing to do.

"Don't be ashamed to need help," Marcus Aurelius wrote.

"Like a soldier storming a wall, you have a mission to accomplish. And if you've been wounded and you need a comrade to pull you up? So what?"

Exactly. *So what?*

You're looking for a hand, not a handout. You're looking for advice. You're not looking to be exempted. You're getting your wounds treated so you can get back into the fight. You're speaking up not for pity or attention but so the same thing doesn't happen to someone else. You're not looking to get an unfair advantage. You're taking advantage of the opportunities and the protections that were designed for precisely the situation you're in.

For years, the addict was afraid to ask for help, afraid to admit their powerlessness. For years, the executive sat behind their desk, struggling with imposter syndrome, afraid to ask if anyone else felt the same way. For years, the mother sat with the black dog of depression, there for her children, afraid to demand that someone be there for her too. For years, the veteran kept their pain to themselves, hiding the true cost of their heroism, afraid of looking weak.

We are afraid to open up. We are scared to share. We don't want anyone to know how we're feeling inside . . . and so all of us feel more alone. What strength it takes to beat back this fear. What pain is caused by the inability or the unwillingness to do so.

When the student asks a question, what happens? They learn

something they didn't know. When the friend reveals a vulnerability to another, what happens? The friendship gets stronger. When the employee admits the workload is too much, what happens? A hire is made and the company gets more efficient. When somebody has the courage to speak about something shameful that was done to them? Society is propelled into action. Someone can help them stop it.

Sometimes just the ask itself is a breakthrough. The admission unlocks something within. Now we're powerful enough to solve our problem.

We are as sick as our secrets. We are at the mercy of fears we dare not articulate, paralyzed by assumptions we refuse to put to the test.

It's okay to need a minute. It's okay to need a helping hand. To need reassurance, a favor, forgiveness, whatever. Need therapy? Go! Need to start over? Okay! Need to steady yourself on someone's shoulder? Of course!

You won't get any of this if you don't ask. You won't get what you're afraid to admit you need. So ask now, right now, while you have the courage. Before it's too late.

We're in this mission together. We're comrades. Ask for help. It's not just brave, it's the *right thing to do.*

When We Rise Above . . .

Fear, before you're actually in the battle, is a normal emotional reaction. It's the last step of preparation, the not-knowing... This is where you'll prove you're a good soldier. That first fight—that fight with yourself—will have gone. Then you will be ready to fight the enemy.

ARMY LIFE (HANDBOOK), 1944

There is a reason to fear.

A logic to it. Or else, physiologically, it wouldn't exist.

Putting self-preservation above all else does have the benefit—above all else—of tending to keep you alive.

But the question is not, Is there a benefit to fear? Of course there is. The question is, What would things look like if everyone acted out of fear all the time?

We know that answer. It would be hell. Life would become—if we can imagine it—even scarier.

So while the reasonable man adapts himself to the world, as

George Bernard Shaw said, progress—hope—depends on the courage of the unreasonable man. It makes sense to fear. To avoid risk. To accommodate. To settle. Self-serving, but certainly safe.

We have countless expressions reminding us: The tall poppy gets cut down. Go with the grain, not against it. You can't beat City Hall.

And yet? If everyone believed this, if fear ruled supreme, not only would those expressions become effective truths, but good would never triumph over evil, new would never break through the status quo, and nothing would ever be improved.

That can't be what we want. That can't be what we were put on this planet to do.

Some people, sure. But not you.

We choose what voice we will listen to. We choose whether we'll play it safe, think small, be afraid, conform, hide, or be cynical. We choose whether we will break these fears down, whether we'll go our own way, whether we look down over the side of the narrow bridge and turn back—or keep going.

To have courage? To brave fear? That's our call. We don't have to do it.

But we can't escape the fact that it is the thing upon which every other good thing depends.

What we want in life, what the world needs—all of it is on the other side of fear. All of it is accessed through courage, should we choose to wield it.

PART II
COURAGE

O to struggle against great odds, to meet enemies
  undaunted!
To be entirely alone with them, to find how much one can
  stand!
To look strife, torture, prison, popular odium, face to
  face!
To mount the scaffold, to advance to the muzzles of guns
  with perfect nonchalance!
To be indeed a God!

WALT WHITMAN

Courage is the management of and the triumph over fear. It's the decision—in a moment of peril, or day in and day out—to take ownership, to assert agency, over a situation, over yourself, over the fate that everyone else has resigned themselves to. We can curse the darkness, or we can light a candle.

We can wait for someone else to come and save us, or we can decide to stand and deliver ourselves. Which will it be? Every hero faces this choice. Our *discrimen*—the critical turning point. The moment of truth. Will you be brave? Will you put yourself out there? What will you reveal your character to be? If cowardice is failure to do your duty, then courage is the decision to step up and do it. Answering the call. Overriding fear and seizing your destiny. Doing the thing you cannot do because it needs to be done . . . with fortitude and spirit, guts and grit, even if you have no idea if you'll succeed. This will not be easy. But we cannot fear. We must, as Shakespeare said, "meet the time as it seeks us." Our destiny is here. Let's seize it.

The Call We Answer . . .

~

One man saved France.

Charles de Gaulle thought it worth saving, and he alone made it so.

As the country fell to Germany in June 1940, as it was overrun not just by tanks but by the fear of its own leaders who quietly and quickly negotiated a surrender with the worst aggressor in modern history, de Gaulle boarded a small plane to England.

It was one of the most frightful flights of his life. Not just because he could have easily been shot down or caught before takeoff, nor because many other flights, including one intended for his family, would crash and kill all on board. "I appeared to myself," he would reflect on that short hour-and-a-half journey, "alone and deprived of everything, like a man on the edge of an ocean that he was hoping to swim across. . . . I felt that a life was ending, a life that I had lived in the framework of a solid France and an indivisible army."

De Gaulle was not France's elected leader. He had no royal blood. He was not even its highest-ranking general. He was more than a citizen, of course. Recently promoted to brigadier general and undersecretary of defense, he had been the only one urging the prime minister that France must fight its way back from the abyss. At the same time, he was also just a man. A man who wasn't ready to give up, wasn't ready for his country to give up.

So he didn't.

Meeting with Churchill shortly after crossing the Channel and landing in England, de Gaulle was offered a chance to speak on the BBC the following day. He commanded no armies, possessed almost no money, had no plan, had no authority to create one, and somehow won.

It has been said that "one man with courage makes a majority," and so it went with de Gaulle.

"I tell you nothing is lost for France," he would say in that famous broadcast. "The same means that conquered us can one day bring us victory. For France is not alone! She is not alone! She is not alone!"

And yet she *was* alone.

De Gaulle's broadcast had been intended mainly for the thousands of French soldiers who had been evacuated by the British. He was calling them to fight with him, to fight for their country. Instead, the vast majority of them asked to be repatriated home, to the Vichy Republic established by the Nazis. De Gaulle's old mentor and boss, General Philippe Pétain—France's great hero in World War I—collaborated with the

Germans and used his reputation to legitimize it. What was the point of fighting on? Who could stop Hitler's inexorable march?

In his sound check for the broadcast, de Gaulle had uttered just one word: *France.* He earnestly, sincerely, beyond logic and facts, believed in that nation. He believed that Pétain's surrender was illegitimate. This was his lodestar, however beyond reason it was. He believed France could be saved.

The facts were grim: de Gaulle, his brave wife and family who had escaped without aid, and a few officers (whom Churchill chose to back with the power of Britain) were all France had left . . .

Would it be enough?

"In every fundamental thing you have done, weren't you always a minority?" the writer and Resistance leader André Malraux would ask de Gaulle at the end of his life.

"I was in a minority, I agree," de Gaulle replied. But, he said, "I knew that, sooner or later, I should cease to be so."

Napoleon, perhaps the only other French hero whose accomplishments don't pale in comparison to de Gaulle's, famously said that "nothing is lost while courage remains." De Gaulle had the courage to call for the ball—to accept the burden of leadership on his shoulders, to resist the pull of hopelessness and choose instead, with animal-like ferocity, the path of a fighter, of someone who would not be broken.

Just as in our time, in the mid-twentieth-century belief in that old theory of the great man of history was low. Could one person really change the world? Can we really make a difference? Or must we concede to the overwhelming forces of time and trend?

"The intervention of human will in the chain of events has something irrevocable about it," de Gaulle had written before the war. "Responsibility presses down with such weight that few men are capable of bearing it alone. That is why the greatest qualities of intelligence do not suffice. Undoubtedly intelligence helps, and instinct pushes one, but in the last resource a decision has a moral element."

But we cannot discount the physical element. De Gaulle was tried in absentia by the Vichy regime and sentenced to death. In the last war, he had been wounded multiple times (including by bayonet), he had been a prisoner of war, and he had attempted to escape, relentlessly, fearlessly, at grave risk. Imagine the courage of his wife, too, commandeering a spot on a boat, getting three young children, including one with Down syndrome, safely to London as enemies swarmed to find her. In the decades to come, de Gaulle and his wife were the victims of *thirty* serious assassination attempts. After one, their car riddled with machine-gun fire, the windows shattered, all the tires blown out, Yvonne emerged, unscathed, and calmly inquired about the groceries she'd recently put in the trunk. De Gaulle mocked his assassins' aim, saying, "These people shoot like pigs." This was a family that mastered fear, transcended it even.

Since we know that de Gaulle was ultimately victorious, we

have chosen to remember that France was united in resistance to its occupiers. This is sadly not the case. People were afraid. They made excuses. They looked at the odds and told themselves it was hopeless. They were willing—shockingly so, in fact—to accept Hitler's bridle and yoke themselves to the Nazi cause if it meant that normal life could quickly resume. French labor was used to power the German war machine. Countless French Jews were sent off to die.*

It is the cowardice of others that creates the opportunities for the individual hero. "When events become grave, and peril pressing," de Gaulle had written in the 1920s, "a sort of tidal wave pushes men of character into the front rank." Now the events for him were grave and pressing, just as they might be for you. He was ready to answer the call. More, he was *putting out the call,* to anyone and everyone who was willing to join him.

Some people run away. Some people stand up. It's that simple.

De Gaulle's courage was in part what inspired the French Resistance. It also indicted, implicitly and explicitly, his countrymen who lacked the courage to fight. Hitler led by fear. Like a devil, he encouraged the absolute worst in people. This was what made de Gaulle so glorious: He made no promises—only demands. It was your *duty* to resist, he said. We are being called

---

* One shudders to think what might have happened to de Gaulle's beloved special needs daughter, Anne, had they stayed in France.

by a higher power, to a higher cause. We must *free ourselves*. In the end, some four hundred thousand French men and women joined this resistance, blowing up bridges, gathering intelligence, sabotaging their occupiers, saving people from the camps, picking off the enemy one by one, weakening them in advance of the Allied invasion.

That is the thing about courage: Just like fear, it is contagious. It was de Gaulle's commitment, his undauntedness, that rallied not just France but the whole world behind him. As René Pleven, one of the first French politicians to join de Gaulle's cause, wrote to his own wife, "I assure you that when one sees all those who have *run away* one feels proud facing the danger." A British report explained, "General de Gaulle symbolizes that France which did not despair, which did not give in. He acted alone."

In June 1944, more than two million Allied troops landed in France. In August, Paris was liberated. It had been four long years in the desert, a darkness endured into a bright dawn. "Paris! Paris outraged! Paris broken! Paris martyred! But Paris *liberated*!" de Gaulle said in his victory speech. "Liberated by itself, liberated by its people with the help of the French armies, with the support and the help of all France, of the France that fights, of the only France, of the real France, of the eternal France!"

A radio reporter in the crowd noted not just the catharsis of the moment, but the drama of the moment in real time. For the war was not yet won. Enemy troops lay just out of sight. Gunshots cracked. Explosions sounded. But de Gaulle shrugged it all off.

"That was one of the most dramatic scenes I have ever seen," Robert Reid reported breathlessly for the BBC. "Firing started all over the place. . . . General de Gaulle was trying to control the crowds rushing into the cathedral. He walked straight ahead into what appeared to me to be a hail of fire. . . . But he went straight ahead without hesitation, his shoulders flung back, and walked right down the center aisle, even while the bullets were pouring about him. It was the most extraordinary example of courage I have ever seen. . . . There were bangs, flashes all about him, yet he seemed to have an absolutely charmed life."

And then de Gaulle headed down the Champs-Élysées for a parade with more than a million of his French compatriots.

He had acted alone until, exactly as he prophesied, he was no longer alone.

Courage had triumphed over evil. One man had made a majority.

Still, it is essential that we understand that courage is more than just the stand. It's more than just the choice of Hercules, between the easy road and the hard one. One then has to *walk* that hard road.

It was a long journey from those desperate days after the fall of France. There were radio broadcasts, a state built in exile. De Gaulle had to slowly, steadily regain control of the far-flung governments of France's empire. He had to raise money, find generals, outmaneuver political enemies, wage a public relations battle. He had to consult with the Allies on their strategy, and when he was not consulted, he would bang his fists and shout and raise such a stink that they were forced to bring him back to the table. He had to stand down snipers even as he stood celebrating the liberation.

"What everyone seems to ignore," de Gaulle would say, "is the incredible mixture of patience, of slow development, of obstinate creativity, of trick questions, the dizzying succession of calculation, negotiations, conflicts, trips that we had to carry out to accomplish our enterprise."

It was these traits—each one of them a different form of courage—that transformed France, which had been brought so low, into one of the victorious powers by the end of the war. France *still exists*—that's what de Gaulle insisted. That's what his bravery helped prove. He willed into being a story that ensured the survival of his country. He refused to let them die before their time. He spoke so earnestly of France's greatness that his words became true.

Was de Gaulle at times egotistical? Did he make mistakes? Did he make enemies? Was he divisive and polarizing? Absolutely. He drove Churchill mad. He was regarded with suspicion by Roosevelt. Later, as president of the France he saved, he was maddening to all sorts of people and groups, from the United Nations, to both sides of the Algerian conflict, to all of Canada after his infamous "Vive le Québec libre!" speech, to U.S. president after U.S. president—Truman, Eisenhower, Kennedy, Johnson. There's no question that de Gaulle was difficult to work with, difficult to control, and impossible to intimidate. *Why do you think so many people tried to kill him?* But this independence, this fearlessness was the key to his greatness—as it is the key to most greatness.

"They think perhaps I am not someone easy to work with," de Gaulle would say, shrugging off criticism like Serpico. "But if I were, I would today be in Pétain's general staff." The kind of person who goes their own way, who refuses to accept defeat, who believes faithfully in their own agency, who is brave enough to assert their autonomy even at the risk of death or dissolution is not the kind of person who is easy to boss around or force to compromise.

Of course, de Gaulle was never actually alone as he stood against Germany. Not only because of his allies—allies like the British and Americans whom he did not always credit—but because no one who acts with courage is ever alone.

"I am a man who belongs to nobody," he said, "and belongs to everybody." De Gaulle believed he was playing a role in a grand story, a grand tradition. Along with his comrades, he was just one more actor in the long story of France, "following on from those who have served France since the dawn of her History," he told the Free French, "preceding all those who will serve her for the eternity of her future" so that one day "we will say to France, simply, like Péguy, 'Mother, look upon your sons who have fought for you.'"

He was on the Hero's Journey. He was answering the same call that his ancestors had answered, that you yourself have the opportunity to answer—if you refuse to be afraid, if you seize your destiny.

Churchill called de Gaulle *l'homme du destin*—the man of destiny. When we follow our destiny, when we seize what is meant to be ours, we are never alone. We are walking alongside Hercules. We are following in the footsteps of the greats. We are guided by God, by the gods, by a guiding spirit, the same one that guided de Gaulle and Napoleon, Joan of Arc, Charlemagne, and every other great man and woman of history.

Courage may call for us to stand alone, alone against the incredible adversity, even against what feels like the entire world.

But we are not afraid, because we are not actually alone when we take that stand.

For behind us, as there was for de Gaulle, there is a great empire.

And we must know that if we fight hard and long enough, we will find *everyone* is with us.

The World Wants to Know

~

Varlam Shalamov was sentenced in 1937 to years of hard labor in a Soviet gulag.

What were his crimes?

The same crimes that brought most people to those frozen hellholes: Falling on the wrong side of a totalitarian regime. Random bad luck. Daring to criticize the powers that be. For not being communist *enough*. For not confessing, though that hardly would have saved him.

There he was in one of the darkest places a human could be, and what did he find? He found out quite a lot about the human condition. "I discovered that the world should be divided not into good and bad people but into cowards and non-cowards," he wrote. "Ninety-five percent of cowards are capable of the vilest things, lethal things, at the mildest threat."

When we ask about courage, we are thinking about it precisely wrong.

It's not our question to ask.

For it is *we* who are being asked the question.

In Cormac McCarthy's dark and beautiful novel *All the Pretty Horses*—in a prison not unlike the one that Shalamov actually occupied—Emilio Perez puts the question to John Grady like this:

> "The world wants to know if you have cojones. If you are brave?"

The world is asking *you* about your courage. Every minute of every day. Your enemies are asking you this question. Your obstacles are too.

Because we need to know. Are you one of the cowards? Are you someone we can count on? Do you have what it takes?

Seneca would say that he actually pitied people who have never experienced misfortune. "You have passed through life without an opponent," he said. "No one can ever know what you are capable of, not even you."

That's why this question is so important. The world wants to know what category to put you in, so it sends difficult situations your way. These are not inconveniences or even tragedies but opportunities, as questions to answers: *Do I have cojones?* Or perhaps, less gendered, *Do I have a spine? Am I brave? Am I going to face this problem or run away from it? Will I stand up or be rolled over?*

You answer this question not with words but with actions. Not privately but publicly.

If Not You, Then Who?

~

For thousands of years human beings have found themselves here, forced to ask themselves another famous question, adapted from the rabbi Hillel:

"If not me, then who? If not now, then when?"

Or as John Lewis put it:

"If not *us,* then who?"

Because it does have to be done. At one of the darkest points of the Civil War, as he laid a months-long siege to the city of Petersburg—the only remaining obstacle in front of the Confederate capitol of Richmond—Ulysses S. Grant said, "The task is a big one and has to be performed by someone." It took almost nine months against an entrenched and desperate enemy, but Grant refused to be deterred. He would not waver. He would not be distracted, he would not push the responsibility onto someone else or fall prey to fantasies of some less costly solution.

No. He sat there. He dug in. He *led.* In taking Petersburg, he did what so many other generals had failed to do, just in the nick of time. Within weeks, the South would surrender. It had been an enormous task—but in facing it instead of fleeing from it, finally, the mighty scourge of war was ended.

In 1861 Oliver Wendell Holmes was a scion of a rich, powerful family. He could have hired a substitute to fight for him in the Civil War. Instead, he enlisted and fought and nearly died during several battles. After law school and a lucrative private practice, he secured a cushy job at Harvard that he could have held for the rest of his life, safe in the pleasurable cocoon of the world of ideas. Instead, he left that job—at no small expense in money and relationships—to take a state judgeship because he believed that lawyers ought to go where the law was being made. Later, he was elevated to the Supreme Court, where he served tirelessly until he was ninety years old—a record for the court.

"I think that, as life is action and passion," Holmes would write, "it is required of a man that he should share the passion and action of his time at peril of being judged not to have lived."

"Who am I that I should go to the Pharaoh?" Moses asked when destiny called. The answer for him is the same as it is for you: *The right person for the right job.*

Each of us is unique. Grant was. Holmes was. Nightingale

and de Gaulle were. Each of us has our own skills, our own set of experiences and insights. We each receive our call. If we don't answer it, then we deprive the world of something. Our failure of courage ripples out beyond us, into the lives of other people.

Because if you don't adopt that kid, who will? If you don't start that business, who will? If you don't finally say those three magic words today, when will you?

Likely no one, likely never. And if someone does, it won't be you—it will be different. It will not be as good. It will not be what *you* bring to the table.

The belief that an individual can make a difference is the first step. The next is understanding that *you* can be that person.

Preparation Makes You Brave

~

Are other people naturally braver than you? Or are they just better prepared?

"Know-how is a help," opens the *Army Life* handbook that the U.S. Army brass handed to each of its millions of soldiers in the Second World War. "There is more mental comfort," it continues, "more personal satisfaction, in knowing your place and part in this Army than in any other single thing you can now do for yourself. Be selfish about it, if you like; learn your job because knowing how to handle yourself will make you feel better. A knowledge of your duties and obligations, your rights and opportunities, will one day make you more valuable to the Army. That, too, will give you a *personal* satisfaction in the long run."

Although fear can be explained away, it's far more effective to replace it. With what? *Competence.* With training. With tasks. With a job that needs to be done.

So it went with the Roman army when they were trapped in the Caudine Forks in 321 BC. Barricaded in a narrow pass by felled trees piled with rocks on one end and by armed men on the heights on the other end, the troops were hopelessly trapped. As the magnitude of their predicament sunk in—surrounded on all sides by insuperable obstacles and a dug-in enemy—they were numb with fear. Each man looked around at the next, assuming he might know what to do. The generals too were lost in a stupor. How could this have happened? What could be done? How could they possibly survive?

Then one soldier, nameless, anonymous, lost to history, made the first move toward setting up fortifications. Instinctually, without orders, the other men followed. Sure, it seemed utterly pointless to build a stockade given the desperate nature of their position, but doing something was better than nothing. They let their training take over—they found solace and strength in it.

It was mental comfort. It was something to occupy the time. It was *their job*. The enemy, watching this strange behavior, began to jeer and taunt. The Romans themselves laughed at their own fruitless labor but continued. Indeed, in fortifying their positions the Romans fortified themselves. The stupor they found themselves in soon lifted, and their resolve hardened. The enemy soon made terms with the Romans rather than risk attacking such a disciplined foe.

Training is not just something that athletes and soldiers do. It is the key to overcoming fear in any and all situations. What we do not expect, what we have not practiced, has an advantage over us. What we have prepared for, what we have anticipated, we will be able to answer. As Epictetus says, the goal when we experience adversity is to be able to say, "This is what I've trained for, for this is my discipline."

If you don't want to flinch when it comes, Seneca would say around the same time, *train before it comes*.

What we are familiar with, we can manage. Danger can be mitigated by experience and by good training. Fear leads to aversion. Aversion to cowardice. Repetition leads to confidence. Confidence leads to courage.

The bully who must be confronted. The difficult press conference. The risky bet. The unpopular but ethical stand. Being surrounded by enemies on all sides. These are the moments when our training must kick in, because if it doesn't, fear will. Doubt will. Minding our own business, taking the easy road, that's what we will instinctively do.

To borrow a famous phrase from Allen Iverson: We're talking about *practice?* Yes, we're talking about practice. Because it's the most important thing. With practice, you go through the actions in your mind. You build the muscle memory of what you do in this situation or that one. You learn how to fortify and are fortified in the process. You run through the drills, you play your scales. You have someone ask you purposely tough questions. You get comfortable with discomfort. You train at your T-pace for deliberate intervals, raising your threshold as a runner. You familiarize. You assemble your rifle with a blindfold on, you work out with a weight vest on. You do it a thousand times, and then a thousand times more while there is no pressure so that when there is, you'll know exactly what to do.

Know-how is a help. But it's preparation that makes you brave.

Just Start Somewhere.
Just Do Something.

~

The journey to whistleblowing began for Daniel Ellsberg by attending a peace conference. By asking a few questions. By deciding to take the documents home to really look at them.

Nobody starts by leaking the Pentagon Papers. It's always less dramatic than that. The French speak of *petites actions*—those first small steps, the builders of momentum, the little things that add up.

We would do well to think of that concept when we feel afraid or when we despair in the face of an enormous problem.

We don't need to lead a grand charge.

Put aside thoughts of some death-defying gesture.

Sometimes the best place to start is somewhere small.

Indeed it was for Ellsberg, who was working for an administration that did not tolerate dissent of any stripe, including the asking of pointed and uncomfortable questions. Leaking the papers to the *New York Times* wasn't what he had in mind at the beginning either—it was a gradual escalation after his other, more traditional efforts pointed him in that direction.

And so it goes for every previously invincible tyrant—from Richard Nixon to Harvey Weinstein and all those who came after—somebody brings them down. Somebody makes the first crack in the armor. Could it be you?

"Never lose an opportunity of urging a practical beginning, however small," Florence Nightingale said, "for it is wonderful how often in such matters the mustard-seed germinates and roots itself." So it went for her. It was working in one hospital for one summer that gave her the confidence to dedicate her life to the task. It was much easier to convince her family not to stop her when she claimed her nursing experiment had an expiration date. It was easier to convince herself too.

Thomas Edison disagreed; he said that life was too short to start at the small end of things. He always wanted to go for the hard problems, the ambitious projects. *Fortune favors the bold*, right?

Perhaps the way to align these ideas is that we can indeed begin with *petites actions* but on our magnum opus.

Start small . . . on something big.

Eliminate one problem. Move things one iota. Write one sentence. Send one letter. Make a spark.

We can figure out what's next after that.

Your headlights illuminate just a few feet of the dark road in front of you, and yet that is enough for you to move forward and make continual progress.

Isn't that how we solve big problems? By breaking them

down? By focusing on the piece in front of us? Ideally, early on, before it gets harder or buried in other problems? (Rivers are more easily forded at their source, goes the expression.) Build some momentum, some confidence as you begin crossing stuff off the list. And most of all, isn't this what training helps you with? Telling you the first and smallest thing you should do— what your job in this moment happens to be.

You will not always be successful, but then again, it's not *all* about you anyway. Someone can pick up where you left off. All you have to do is get things started. All you have to do is handle your part of the relay to the best of your ability. Do your best, do what you can, do it right now. That's it.

There's no way around it, though—you'll have to take action. But you'll be surprised at what a difference making a small difference can make.

"He who does *something* at the head of one regiment," Abraham Lincoln reminds us, "will eclipse him who does *nothing* at the head of a hundred." Better to win a small battle than continually to defer for some larger, perfect battle in the future.*

The struggle continues. We play our part.

We get started. We do what we can, where we are, with what we have. It adds up.

---

*Lincoln fired General George B. McClellan for this reason, leaving the general-in-chief position unfilled rather than keep a timid leader. When he eventually promoted Grant, the motive was simple. "He *fights*," Lincoln said.

Go!

~

There were all the reasons in the world for Charles Lindbergh not to go.

No one had ever successfully flown nonstop across the Atlantic. He himself had never even done an over-water flight before. Never really flown long-distance at all. Never flown more than five hundred miles without the safety net of a strong tailwind and the ability to navigate against landmarks on the ground. Never even stayed up the fifty-five consecutive hours it would take to complete the flight.

Then one of his rivals crashed on a trial flight, seriously injuring three of the four crew members. A few weeks later, two pilots trying to cross from Paris to New York disappeared mid-flight and were never heard from again.

And he was supposed to do this—make it thirty-six hundred miles across open, featureless water—*alone*? In a plane whose load was so precarious he couldn't afford the twenty extra pounds for a parachute? The world sure was asking a lot of him, more even than he was asking of himself.

On May 19, 1927, Lindbergh arrived at Roosevelt Field on Long Island and saw no signs of any of his competitors. There was a brief break in the weather. He filled up his tanks. He had trouble going to sleep that night. In the morning, there were more logistical issues. Arguments about the wind. He was running late. All the objections and difficulties came rushing back to his mind. The eyes of the men in the hangar and on the tarmac were filled with doubt—they had witnessed this scene so many times.

He climbed into the wicker seat. He put on his goggles. He started the engine. In a few minutes, he was taxiing toward destiny. He hesitated. Considered it all again. Pushed it all aside and accelerated. At 7:52 a.m., his wheels lifted off the ground, with just twenty feet of runway to spare. In less than a day and a half, he'd be standing on the ground in France.

How do you get over all that fear? All those reasons not to do whatever it is you set out to do?

In the words of the decorated Navy SEAL Jocko Willink, to get over the fear, *you go.*

You just do. You leap into the dark. It is the only way.

Because if you don't, what looms? Failure. Regret. Shame. A lost opportunity. Any hope of moving forward.

"In matters like this," de Gaulle once explained to some reticent members of his administration, "one must move or die. I have chosen to move; that does not exclude the possibility of also dying." And so he went, and so his wife went, as France was falling—no suitcases, no parachute, no backup plan. He went courageously forward like this dozens of other times in his career, whether it was in the Algerian crisis or the student protests of 1968.

Alea iacta est.

*Damn the torpedoes!**

Are there risks? Of course. It's not unreasonable to be worried about them. But there is no chance of success if you do nothing, if you don't even try. No one can guarantee safe passage in life, nothing precludes the possibility of failing or dying.

But if you don't go? Well, you ensure failure and suffer a different kind of death.

Later, you're going to wish you did something. We always do.

Which means, right now, *you gotta go.*

---

* In the Civil War, naval mines were referred to as "torpedoes." This famous expression didn't mean "arm your weapons" as some think, but instead, "Forget the obstacles, let's proceed!"

Speak Truth to Power

~

Decimus Laberius was ordered by Julius Caesar to perform for him.

To some, this would have been an honor. To others, a minor indignity.

To Decimus, no bootlicker, it created a moral obligation.

A moral obligation for defiance.

There, with Caesar in the audience, with everyone watching, Decimus harangued Caesar to his face, mocking his tyranny and predicting his painful demise. More impressive still, he did it so well, so artfully, so boldly that Caesar was helpless to punish him for it.

The Greek word for this kind of courage was *parrhesia*. It was the speaking of truth to power. It was refusing to buy the lie or to play it false. Socrates was the classic *parrhesiastes*, a man who said what others were afraid to say to the people they were afraid to say it to. To paraphrase an ancient historian: No one could make Socrates do, say, or think anything that was alien to his character.

In a sense, it's strange that we even admire this. Shouldn't that be the norm? Isn't that our basic duty as people?

To know the truth and not say the truth . . . this is to betray the truth.

You may escape guilt by staying silent, but there is no excuse. You're culpable. You're a coward. It may be that no one *wants* to hear the truth, and they may very well be scared to hear it, but you can't be afraid to say it.

In 1934, Dietrich Bonhoeffer, the German pastor and theologian, came late to the children's story "The Emperor's New Clothes." Having watched his fellow Christians start lying to themselves about Hitler, having watched the beginning of Hitler's heinous lies, the story hit him like a ton of bricks. "All we are lacking today," he wrote in a letter to his brother, "is the child who speaks up at the end."

If the boy in that story can instinctively, naturally defy a king, what's your excuse?

Of course, you have a million: It would hurt your job. People won't like you. It wouldn't make that much of a difference. It will set your work back. Nobody wants to hear it. You don't want to get on their bad side.

Okay, *bootlicker.*

Look, it's one thing to be intimidated. It's another to debase yourself.

That's what de Gaulle realized about Hitler. That his force was entirely dependent on the "cowardice of others." No one was willing to call the bully a bully. No one in Germany was willing to see that the emperor had no clothes, and was in fact a raving, murderous lunatic. They definitely weren't willing to say so. Because no one said anything, no one did anything except tell Hitler what he wanted to hear. And so they all became complicit.

Still, it must be stipulated that the obligation to tell the truth is not a license to be cruel. Socrates was trying to help people get to what mattered. His intention was not to offend, only to teach. But that he did offend some people, that he did make some enemies? That didn't stop him from the pursuit of wisdom nor put him off his duty.

Society cannot function without this type of character. It's not always so serious as looking Caesar in the eye and telling him what they think of him. It's also Dave Chappelle making fun of our hypocrisies and our absurdities. It's Nassim Taleb puncturing our pretentions and certainties. It's Diogenes, questioning our most basic assumptions.

We need people to challenge the status quo. We need artists who probe personal issues . . . and make public critiques. We need politicians who insist on leading from a place of honesty, and they themselves need expert advisers who do not hesitate to tell them unpleasant facts. We need a population that refuses to tolerate propaganda, rationalizations, or cover-ups. People in every station who are willing to stand up and say, "This is not right. I won't be a part of it."

We need *you* to say that.

Be the Decider

～

Imprinted in the memory of future secretary of state Dean Acheson was General George Marshall's mastery of leadership. Diplomats and leaders wanted to debate forever. About what to do. About who was at fault. About what to say. About what to have for lunch.

Inevitably, Marshall cut through with a command: "Gentlemen, don't fight the problem! Decide it!"

Because while fear wants you to spend the day in deliberation, courage knows that won't be possible.

The rarest of all the gifts from the Gods, Acheson realized, was *the ability to decide*. To succeed in life, in foreign policy, in a complicated and messy world, a leader must learn how to make decisions with courage and clarity. No equivocation. No vacillation.

Marshall had that. So did Truman. It was how they were able to save postwar Europe from starvation and bankruptcy, as well as aiding Berlin after it was blockaded by Russia. They were willing to step up and choose.

"Your job as president is to decide," Acheson wrote. "Mr. Truman *decided.*"

In the first thirty days of his presidency alone, Truman had to make decisions about:

- Soviet interference in Poland
- The first meeting of the United Nations
- The first shipment of uranium
- Soviet entry into the war against Japan

Within weeks and months, he'd also be deciding whether to drop the atomic bomb, whether to save Europe via the Marshall Plan, whether to implement the doctrine of containment against Soviet aggression, whether to go ahead with the Berlin Airlift, and on and on and on.

You might think that these were agonizing, difficult decisions, given the stakes and the lack of consensus among the experts. They were.

But that was only part of it. Truman and Marshall knew they would be criticized. They knew that each decision was a risk. They knew that the buck stopped with them—that their name would be on the decision, literally in the case of the Truman Doctrine or the Marshall Plan.

Yet they not only decided, but they decided and focused on the scariest thing there is in this life: Following through on your decisions.

The doctor in the operating room cannot delay, they must make their decisions quickly, they must act on them and have the courage to face the life-and-death results of the performance. The fighter, the trader, the performer, the CEO at a company in turnaround—every leader is in the same bind. There is a savagery to these professions, where consequences hang in the balance. A strike at the jugular is needed, people must be laid off, checks must be written. There is something awful about this savagery—but no one gains, least of all the vulnerable people at stake, by tarrying or timidity.

We claim we debate so we can get to the right decision, that we need more information. In truth, we are delaying. We don't want to leave the comfort of the status quo. We don't want to have to own the consequences.

We're debating leaving our job, whether to make this investment or that one, whether we're going to go public with what we know, whether we're going to let somebody go . . . We put it off, over and over again, avoiding the crux of what we need to be *doing* in favor of considering endless what-ifs or distractions.

Decimus, as he strode off the stage, having courageously confronted Caesar, mocked Cicero to his face as well, calling him the man who "sits on two stools," a reference to Cicero's failure to choose a side in the civil war. Soon enough, Cicero's enemies made the choice for him.

There's a great expression: Whatever you're not changing, you're *choosing*. Later, you're going to wish you did something.

Whether it's leaving an abusive relationship or starting a company, don't fight it—*decide it*. Now.

These precious seconds you spent debating could have gotten you farther away from the hurricane. The time you spent hemming and hawing about speaking up could have been put toward mitigating the fallout. The best time to have tackled a hard problem was a long time ago; the second best time is now.

"Things look black," Truman wrote to his daughter in 1948 as the Soviets clamped down in Czechoslovakia. "A decision will have to be made and I am going to make it."

You can't beat a problem by debating it, only by deciding what you're going to do about it and then *doing it*. Not a decision for decision's sake, of course, but the right call, *right now*. And if your decision happens to be wrong, or you make a mistake, then decide again, with the same kind of courage and clarity.

It's Good to Be "Difficult"

~

As she sat across the table from her job interviewer after several rounds of interviews, the research chemist just barely made out the evaluation written at the top of the paper. Reading as best she could upside down, Margaret Thatcher saw what they thought of her:

> "This young woman has much too strong a personality to work here."

There were two ways to read it: as an indictment or as high praise.

The coward picks the former and listens. With confidence, such criticism can be politely ignored. It takes courage to power past it, to not let it—or them—change you.

So what will it be?

Remember what they said about Serpico.

What they said about de Gaulle.

What they said about Nightingale.

You're difficult.

Of course they were. The well-behaved rarely make history. Had these men and women been a little more conciliatory, a little more willing to accept the role expected of them, had they cared a little bit more about what other people thought, were they a little bit easier to deter, there wouldn't have been an independent stand to take in the first place.

And while the powers that be might have called these people difficult, history has come to call them something else: *iconoclasts.*

Some of us are afraid to be different. Most everyone is afraid to be *difficult.* But there is freedom in those traits. Freedom to fight, aggressively, repeatedly, for what we believe in. To insist on a higher standard. To not compromise. To not accept that the "matter has been settled."

It takes courage to do that. Especially in a world that doesn't want to be bothered, that wants everyone to stay in their lane, that doesn't want anyone asking *why.*

August Landmesser wasn't thinking about history when he refused to give the mandated Nazi salute at the unveiling of a new German navy vessel. He just knew that he didn't follow rules or conventions that violated his convictions. It was why he married a Jewish woman in 1935 in contravention of the law. He didn't know he was being photographed, that he'd go down in history as a symbol of the lone German who refused to endorse tyranny—the lone man who stood up to the pressure of the mob.

He was difficult. It cost him everything. But he wouldn't have it any other way.

They'll try to punish you. Which is why, day in, day out, you have to defy them. You have to be combative. You have to be determined. You have to be confident. *No,* that's not how this is going to go. *No,* what you're proposing is not "best for everybody." *No,* I am not going to keep my mouth shut. *No,* this isn't over. *No,* I'm not going to "tone myself down."

They're going to call you crazy—because courage *is* crazy. We have to be willing to look that way, to be true to who we are anyway. We can't just not be afraid to be ourselves. We have to *insist on it.*

Despite the costs. Despite the resistance. Despite the fear. It won't be easy, but it will be worth it.

For the difficult know the pleasure of the smirking smile in John Lewis's Mississippi mugshot from 1961. The pleasure of causing *good trouble.* Of being on the right side of things. The pleasure of disruption, and hopefully, ultimately, eventually, the pleasure of good triumphing over evil.

Margaret Thatcher was difficult, probably too difficult to work at that forgettable chemical plant. But it was her stubbornness and her stridency—hardened as it was by conflict with people who resisted it—that eventually equipped her to marshal Britain through a difficult period of modern history. You don't become the first female prime minister of England by blending in.

She was the Iron Lady. Just like Serpico and de Gaulle and Lewis and Nightingale, she couldn't have been anything else. They were called to be who they were, and they had the courage to insist upon answering.

Just a Few Seconds of Courage

~

On October 19, 1960, Martin Luther King Jr. was arrested for trying to eat at a restaurant inside Rich's department store in Atlanta. With their enemy in custody, southern authorities seized the opportunity to try and crush King while they had the chance. Holding him on other charges, they denied bail and sent him to the state prison in Reidsville, where he was to be sentenced to four months on a chain gang. There was real worry that King might be beaten or lynched, and so, overwhelmed with worry, Coretta Scott King, very pregnant with her third child, called both the Nixon and Kennedy campaigns, who, in one of the tightest elections in American history, both desperately needed the black vote.

Nixon, as it happens, was not only friends with King but had personally overseen the Eisenhower administration's civil rights efforts. His advisers urged him to act, but Nixon hesitated—weighing the same considerations that had flashed in the mind of Theodore Roosevelt a half century before. He didn't want to lose the South. He didn't want to wade into the middle of controversy. He was worried it would seem like grandstanding. And so he betrayed King in the moment, and left the door open for Kennedy to call both the governor of Georgia as well as Coretta, whom he rang directly from an airport to console and reassure. Meanwhile, his brother Robert Kennedy called the judge in Alabama and pressured him into releasing King.

King immediately made it known who had been there for him when he needed it, even though he had planned to vote for Nixon. "I had known Nixon longer," he recalled, and "he would call me frequently about things, getting, seeking my advice. And yet, when this moment came, it was like he had never heard of me. So this is why I really considered him a moral coward and one who was really unwilling to take a courageous step and take a risk."

Kennedy went on to win the election two weeks later by less than half a percentage point—just thirty-five thousand key votes across two key states. Two phone calls had won him the presidency. A few seconds of cowardice, the time it would have taken to speak with the wife of a good man wrongly imprisoned, cost Nixon the office.

It doesn't matter who you are or what your track record is. What matters is the moment—sometimes even less than a moment. Do you do it? Or are you too scared?

It takes just a few seconds to hit send on that email . . .

. . . to get those first words out of your mouth

. . . to put your arm in motion to volunteer

. . . to take that first step in the run toward a machine-gun nest

. . . to switch your vote from yes to no or no to yes

. . . to pick up the phone, as Kennedy did, not even to save King's life but to comfort the man's wife.

Once the event is underway, everything else comes naturally. Fulfilling your responsibilities. Putting one foot in front of the other. You drop out of college, then throw yourself into your new career. You file the divorce paperwork and begin rebuilding your life. You walk into the office of the SEC to make your complaint. You'll be too busy to be afraid. Momentum starts working for you—not against you.

There is a great line, in the screenplay written by Cameron Crowe and Matt Damon for the movie *We Bought a Zoo,* based on the true story of a British writer who did exactly that. "You know," Matt Damon's character says to his young son, "sometimes all you need is twenty seconds of insane courage. Just literally twenty seconds of just embarrassing bravery. And I promise you, something great will come of it."

Can we really make such a promise? No, life is not the movies. Results are never certain. You may not succeed, but you do have to try. Because the failure to act? That is a certainty. Those few seconds stick to us like a scarlet letter. "I was afraid" is not an excuse that ages well.

When we marvel at people's courage or are intimidated by it, we often miss that it wasn't some enormous planned-out thing. It began with a simple decision. It began with a leap. "He didn't *know* it was politically sound," King reflected on Kennedy's decision. But the same is true for King—he didn't know when he embarked on that first bus boycott in Montgomery that it would shape the rest of his life as well as the world.

Courage is defined in the moment. In less than *a* moment. When we decide to step out or step up. To leap or to step back.

A person isn't brave, generally. We are brave, specifically.

For a few seconds. For a few seconds of embarrassing bravery we can be great.

And that is enough.

Make It a Habit

~

Harry Burns was an ordinary politician in Tennessee in 1920. He had no history of bold stands or brave votes. He was not a crusader, nor even remotely a political star. He was only twenty-five years old and two years into his term in the state House of Representatives.

"My vote will never hurt you," he reassured his political bosses, who were firmly against ratifying the Nineteenth Amendment, which would enfranchise women. They believed him and he delivered, voting twice to table the discussion of ratification. He even wore a red rose in his lapel, the symbol that the so-called anti-suffragettes used to broadcast their position.

You can imagine the surprise, then, on August 18 when his "aye" not only ratified the amendment in Tennessee but in an instant triggered its passage nationwide, giving the vote to twenty million women. We can imagine the surprise just as we can imagine his terror. Harry was a mama's boy—literally supporting his widowed mother. Mob violence was threatened. His reelection bid was threatened. The majority of constituents were not pleased.

Yet he did it anyway.* It was probably the scariest moment of his life.

We might contrast the tortured bravery of Harry Burns with a similar moment in the life of the politician John McCain. Almost exactly one hundred years after Burns's crisis of conscience, a vote to repeal the Affordable Care Act was held in the U.S. Senate. McCain was a longtime critic of what came to be called "Obamacare"—in fact, he had campaigned on repealing it. But in a dramatic late-night vote, McCain cast the decisive vote—raising his one good arm up and then turning his thumb down sharply to indicate *no*—against the Republican effort to cripple the ACA.

McCain had criticized Democrats in 2010 for their tactics in passing the bill, and he refused to support his own party in doing the same now that they were in power. But why he did it is actually less important for our purposes than *how* he felt doing it.

Even though in both cases the vote took just a "few seconds of courage," it is certain that McCain felt far less trepidation than Harry Burns. He was not conflicted at all. Nor did he waver or question himself. Because he had made a career of surprising

---

* Though we should note that he was only in this position because of the profound and concerted bravery of *generations* of suffragettes.

people. Of being the guy whom everyone is mad at, and sticking with principle even when it's probably not in your best interest.

Burns closed his eyes and leapt into the unknown, probably more than half convinced he was committing career suicide. He'd never done anything like this; he had no experience with the pit in his stomach. He was not steeped in courage. Were it not for a note from his mother, he probably wouldn't have been able to face that moment of fear and doubt. "Hurrah and vote for Suffrage and don't keep them in doubt," she had said. "I noticed Chandlers' speech, it was very bitter. I've been watching to see how you stood but have not seen anything yet. . . . Don't forget to be a good boy and help Mrs. 'Thomas Catt' with her 'Rats.' Is she the one that put rat in ratification, Ha! No more from mama this time . . . With lots of love, Mama."

McCain's mother—still alive at age 105 at the time of the ACA vote—didn't need to remind her son. Because she had raised him to do the harder thing from birth. McCain would write that he learned from her to welcome difficulties as "elements of an interesting life." He had made courage a habit, as we must do. You can see it in his eyes as he walks away having made his decision—there was pleasure in it. He loved delivering that blow, right in the face of his own party's leadership. It was the coup de grâce of his life and career.

We can't just hope to be brave when it counts. It has to be something we cultivate. No athlete just expects to hit the game-winning shot—they practice it thousands of times. They take that shot in scrimmages, in pickup games, alone in the gym as they count down the clock in their head.

There is that clichéd bit of advice: Do one thing each day that scares you.

As it happens, it's not bad. How do you expect to do the big things that scare you—that scare others—if you haven't practiced them? How can you trust that you'll step forward when the stakes are high when you regularly don't do that even when the stakes are low?

So we must test ourselves. We *make courage a habit.*

"*Always* do what you are afraid to do," Ralph Waldo Emerson said. Or as William James wrote, we want to "make our nervous system our ally instead of our enemy." When we make things automatic, then there is less for us to think about—less room for us to do the wrong thing. There is no one, he said, more miserable than the person "in whom nothing is habitual but indecision." In fact there is: No one is more miserable than the person who has made cop-outs and cowardice their go-to decision.

Not only does their daily life suck, but they fail themselves and everyone in the big moments.

The best thing you can do, then, is start with the little things. We can crank the knob in the shower to cold. We can volunteer to address the rowdy audience. We can put on the silly costume to please our kids and not care what anyone thinks. We can admit when we don't know something, at the risk of eye rolls and condescension. We can agree to try what we have never tried before.

And this way we know, when it counts, what to do. We know what we *will* do.

The brave thing. The right thing. The principled thing.

Whatever the consequences.

Seize the Offensive

~

What keeps you up at night?" General James Mattis was once asked by a television reporter.

Before the question was quite finished, he was already answering.

"*I* keep people awake at night."

It was an answer that captured the philosophy by which this warrior—and every warrior before and since—lives their life: A philosophy of *offense*. Of initiative. Of intimidating the enemy rather than being intimidated, of striking fear—striking, *period*—rather than being struck by it. This is why his troops were commanded to set up and sleep in V-shaped camps at night—a V pointed in the direction of the enemy. It's why he famously cashiered an otherwise excellent officer in the Gulf War for going too slow. To borrow a phrase from the British general Sir Douglas Haig, at Mattis's core is the trait that all great soldiers must have: "A sincere desire to engage the enemy." He expects nothing less from his troops.

What, are you going to wait for your opponent to prepare? Are you going to give them an advantage?

No way!

In the civilian world, we call this initiative. In sports, we call it a will to win. And borrowing from the brutal world of war, we get this expression: *killer instinct.*

It is impossible to have a killer instinct without courage. One presupposes the other. And nobody achieves great things—in war, in business, in sports, in life—without either of them.

The Spartans never asked how many of the enemy there were, only *where.* Because they were going to attack anyway. They were in it to win.

In that same campaign where Grant had decided to assume the big task of capturing Petersburg, the one that everyone else had been too afraid to take on, he was repeatedly frustrated by his cautious subordinates, men who had been manhandled by Robert E. Lee and the Confederates for years, while Grant was winning battles in the West. At every turn, they were playing small, reluctant to press, to take the offensive, warning Grant what it was like when Lee really got going.

Grant, who had learned something on the plains of Texas about phantom fears and overestimating the enemy, finally had enough. "Oh, I am heartily tired of hearing about what Lee is going to do," he said to a general who had come to him with more dire predictions. "Some of you always seem to think he is suddenly going to turn a double somersault and land in our rear and on both of our flanks at the same time. Go back to your command, and try to think what we are going to do ourselves, instead of what Lee is going to do."

Thus his order: "Wherever Lee goes, there you will go also." The thing would be pressed. They would not ever go back on the defensive.

As a result, almost exactly a year later, what Lee would be doing was surrendering . . . *to* Grant.

This was the decisive moment of the Civil War—when the North assumed the offensive. Grant decided to stop getting punched and start punching. When Lee held the initiative, the South was strong. The moment he lost it, it became only a matter of time before he lost.

This is true for the most oppressive of opponents. They'll beat on us so long as we let them beat on us. But when we bring the fight to them, when we start choosing our battleground, focusing on where *they* are weak? Now we at least have a shot.

Whatever it is, whatever you're doing, you must pursue it aggressively. When you operate out of fear, when you're on our heels, you have no shot. It's simply not possible to lead that way. To succeed, you must take the offensive. Even when you're being cautious, it must come with the assumption of constant advance, an insistent move toward victory always. You have to demand control of the tempo. You have to *set* the tempo—in battle, in the boardroom, in matters both big and small. You want them to fear what you are going to do, not the other way around.

Stand Your Ground

~

It was on a Monday morning that young Frederick Douglass decided he had had enough.

A notoriously abusive slave breaker named Edward Covey came to punish him, but Douglass grabbed him by the throat. The resistance stunned the overseer, who had never experienced such a thing. Every slave knew that to lay a hand on a white man meant death—and yet here was Douglass, just seventeen years old, beating the hell out of one.

Covey cried for help, but reinforcements were quickly deterred when Douglass kicked the first one hard in the chest. For two hours—two hours!—Douglass and Covey battled there in the yard. Douglass fighting savagely for his life, for his very dignity as a human being; Covey surprised, humiliated, unused to defending himself. In the end, in defeat, exhaustion, and fear, Covey let Douglass go, somehow rationalizing to himself that he had taught the slave a lesson.

"There comes a time when people get tired of being trampled over by the iron feet of oppression," Martin Luther King Jr.

would later say. Douglass decided he was tired that morning in Maryland. It changed everything.

"I felt as I never felt before," he wrote. "It was a glorious resurrection, from the tomb of slavery, to the heaven of freedom. My long-crushed spirit rose, cowardice departed, bold defiance took its place; and I now resolved that, however long I might remain a slave in form, the day had passed forever when I could be a slave in fact."

To understand where the empowered call came from, we must go back to when Douglass was eight and had watched a slave named Nelly be brutally whipped. The overseer, a cruel but confident man, ended up with far more than he bargained for with Nelly, a mother of five children. With her nails and fists, Nelly made even grabbing hold of her difficult. She screamed and yelled. She clawed at the dirt, grabbing everything she could as he dragged her to the whipping post. One of her children even bit him on the leg. "She seemed," Douglass observed, "determined to make her whipping cost the man as much as possible."

By the time the overseer administered the punishment, his bloody face attested to Nelly's success. Even as he whipped her, she was not subdued. She showered him with curses, denounced the evil of slavery and its evildoers. Her skin tore, but her spirit remained unbroken.

The scene implanted itself in the boy's memory and instilled in Frederick Douglass a seed of courage that bloomed out, suddenly, violently that day with his own master, and would bear heroic fruit across some fifty-seven years of public advocacy for justice.

How could anyone ever intimidate Douglass again? How could odds ever deter him? What threats could his enemies possibly make? He had stared down certain death, backed down overwhelming oppression even as a powerless slave. Once you dine on courage—and freedom—and have stood up for yourself, the taste of fear is much harder to tolerate. This is as true for the young couple integrating a lunch counter in 1956 as it is for the meek boy who stands up to the class bully.

"The old doctrine that submission is the best cure for outrage and wrong does not hold good on the slave plantation," Douglass wrote. "He is whipped oftenest who is whipped easiest, and that slave who has the courage to stand up for himself against the overseer, although he may have many hard stripes at the first, becomes in the end a freeman, even though he sustain the formal relation of a slave."

You can kill me but you can't whip me became Douglass's motto. Indeed, he would not be whipped again, becoming as he said, half free the moment he asserted himself. Soon enough, he claimed the rest of his right by braving the slave catchers as he ran away to freedom.

To use another phrase from Martin Luther King Jr., when we straighten our backs, we might be beaten—but we can't be ridden. For Douglass, that meant literally fighting. King and his fellow civil rights activists resisted in a different way, throwing themselves repeatedly against the dogs and the fire hoses and the shotguns of their oppressors until the jails were full and the system collapsed.

We cannot tolerate abuse, constraints, or injustice. We can't hide from our problems. We can only step to them. Submission is no cure. Nor can we expect outrages to magically go away on their own. We must draw the line, somewhere—if not right now, then very soon. We must demand our sovereignty. Insist on it.

Each of us has more power than we know.

And by demanding our rights—by fighting back against oppression or abuse or poor treatment—we're not only being brave, we are, like Douglass, helping everyone who comes after us.

Courage Is Contagious

~

When another country called on Sparta for military help, the Spartans wouldn't send their army. They sent *one* Spartan commander.

This was all it took.

Because courage, like fear, is contagious. One person who knows what they are doing, who isn't afraid, who has a plan is enough to reinforce an outnumbered army, to buck up a broken system, to calm chaos where it has taken root. And so a single Spartan was all their allies needed.

So goes the story about the Texas Ranger Bill McDonald, called in by the authorities in Dallas in the early 1900s to break up an illegal prizefight. When he arrived, the mayor was aghast. "They only sent one ranger?!" he asked. "You only got one riot, don't you?" McDonald replied.

This is the truth of that saying we talked about earlier come to life: *One man with courage makes a majority.*

Because "makes" is the operative word. It doesn't start that way . . . it becomes that way.

You don't have to be a Spartan general or a Texas Ranger to *make* a difference either. The combat historian and U.S. Army officer S. L. A. Marshall would say that "no matter how lowly his rank, any man who controls himself contributes to the control of others. . . . Fear is contagious but courage is not less so."

You don't have to be the smartest guy in the regiment. Or the biggest. Or the best shot. You don't have to have all the answers. You just have to keep yourself in check. You have to do your job in the moment, let your training guide you. You do what's right, what is immediately in front of you, bravely, calmly, clearly.

Whoever you are. Whatever you do.

The citizen who is not distracted by manipulative propaganda helps hold the government accountable, the person who does not make a run on the bank when the market dips helps keep the economy going, the parent who puts on a brave face helps their child fight cancer. Just as the ordinary soldier helps their comrades and hurts the enemy by cinching on their helmet, clenching their chattering teeth, and refusing to consider retreat. As Marshall said, "The courage of any one man reflects in some degree the courage of all of those who are within his vision."

You make a difference when you are brave. Because you make others brave in the process.

Like a virus, calm spreads by contact. It spreads through the air. We *exude it,* shedding our excess strength onto others, infecting them as they in turn infect others—not with a degrading, harmful agent, but one that builds strength and purpose.

When everything is charged with fear, a spark can ignite a panic. It can ensure demoralization and then defeat. But just as easily, one person can ground out this dangerous electrical current. One person can turn things around.

The question for you, then, is are you that person? Are you part of the problem or can you be the solution? Are you the one they call? Or are you the one they have to calm down?

You Have to Own It

~

It's strange how often it happens. An otherwise extraordinarily courageous person turns out to be afraid of the most ordinary thing in the world: responsibility.

Lord Lucan ordered the charge of the Light Brigade. Lord Cardigan commanded it. Together, they sent some six hundred British cavalry against Russian forces in one of the most insanely brave but pointless attacks in military history.

And here are their statements:

"Men, it is a mad-brained trick, but it is no fault of mine."

"I do not intend to bear the slightest particle of responsibility. I gave the order to charge under what I consider a most imperious necessity and I will not bear one particle of the blame."

They could face the merciless bullets of the enemy. They could march in lockstep in the face of enfilading fire. But criticism? Blame? From this, like all weak leaders, they fled. They couldn't even muster up enough courage to question the obviously senseless orders that led to the tragedy, simply passing them along to their men, choosing almost certain death over deciding that the buck stopped with them.

This is the rule: You decided to *go.*

Now you have to own what happens.

No excuses. No exceptions.

That you carry your own weight in this world, that is all we ask. That you own your own actions. Certainly when you're a leader.

The buck stops with you. Always.

"It's not my fault." "It's not my problem." "Don't blame me." These are not phrases that can exist in your vocabulary.

Not if you want to be great. Not unless you're a coward.

"The willingness to accept responsibility for one's own life," Joan Didion observed, "is the source from which self-respect springs."

The perks of leadership come at a cost. The tax on courage is steep. You will take *heat.*

If that bothers you? Then you might be happier doing nothing, saying nothing, being nothing.

Yet we always seem to think we can get away with it, that we can hedge.

A funny wrinkle to the story about the Light Brigade: Alfred, Lord Tennyson, then the poet laureate of the empire, wrote his haunting, inspiring poem about the tragic heroism of the ordinary soldiers in that charge:

> Cannon to right of them,
> Cannon to left of them,
> Cannon in front of them
> Volleyed and thundered;
> Stormed at with shot and shell,
> Boldly they rode and well,
> Into the jaws of Death,
> Into the mouth of hell
> Rode the six hundred.

And do you know how he published it? Under a pseudonym, because *he was worried the poem might not reflect "decorously" on someone in his position.*

We said before that courage is contagious, but you have to be willing to catch it. Tennyson immersed himself in the bravery of those poor soldiers . . . but followed the example of their officers instead.

If you're going to speak out: Sign your name. Sign your name on everything you do. That's the brave—no, the basic—thing to do.

You break it, you buy it. You make the move, you own it. You say it, you stand behind it. You order it, you accept the blame.

This is the source from which self-respect springs and leaders are made.

You Can Always Resist

Commander Jeremiah Denton was selected for a propaganda broadcast.

It had been ten months in the North Vietnamese prison camp now. It had been many long days of cruel interrogations.

As he sat in his chair in front of the cameras, exhausted, hungry, and aching, anticipating the threatened beatings to come, he considered his options. He could say nothing. He could try to answer the questions as banally as possible. He could find a way to pass some loving word back to his family, the wife and seven kids he missed so dearly. He could say all the things the captors wanted him to say and earn himself a nice reprieve, maybe even special treatment for the rest of his time in the so-called Hanoi Hilton.

What he chose instead was an incredible gesture of defiance: Answering the perfunctory questions from his interrogators, Denton began to blink, slowly, as if he were blinded by the lights from the camera.

A long blink.

Three long blinks.

A short blink, a long blink, and a short blink.

A long blink.

Two short blinks, then a long blink.

A short blink, a long blink, and a short blink.

A short blink.

Until he had spelled out *T-O-R-T-U-R-E* in Morse code for all the world to see.

His captors thought they had broken him. Instead, he had broken them, using the actions of his abusers against them, humiliating them on the international stage.

It has been said that a Stoic is someone who says "*Fuck you*" to fate. That's right.

They *resist*. They fight.

They will not be made to do the wrong thing. Especially under pressure.

The corporate attorney who comes by to remind you of your nondisclosure agreement after you just quit in disgust. The entrenched competitor who tells you they're going to bury your little business if you don't accept their offer. The shakedown artist asking for money to go away. The politician who wants your submission. The official who demands that you back off.

It may be explicit. Or it may be subtle. Over a big matter or a small one that nobody cares about but you. Still, the message is clear: *Or else.*

We need to remember the story of the Spartan garrison besieged by King Philip, the brutal father of Alexander the Great. If I get through these walls, he told them, it won't be pretty. If I am victorious, I'll kill every single one of you.

The Spartans replied with one big word: *If.*

As in, we're not going to go easy. As in, you're going to have to back up those words. *You're going to have to beat me first. You can kill me, but you aren't going to whip me.*

Raw defiance. It's an underrated thing. It can go a long way. And if Frederick Douglass and Nelly could muster it, even inside the oppression of chattel slavery, why can't you?

We talked before about how John Adams wanted to put Hercules on the seal of the United States. Ben Franklin proposed a motto for the new republic in a similar vein: "Rebellion to Tyrants is Obedience to God."

Not just to tyrants, but also to bullies, liars, abusers, assholes, frauds, demagogues, cheaters, and bad actors.

Courage says, *Over my dead body.* Courage says, *Not if I can help it.* Courage says, *I'm doing things my way, according to my own code, no matter what you say.*

They can hurt you. They can yell at you. They can do horrible things.

But you are not powerless. In fact, you have more power than you know. "I am too poor to bow," de Gaulle told his British allies. He would not be submissive. He would not tread gently—not to anyone, enemies or friends. He was a fighter, and that's what he was going to do.

You have agency. You have strength. You can make them regret ever tangling with you.

Never accept the foregone conclusion. Only a loser stops battling their opponent before the match is over. Fight for every yard. Fight for *you*.

No one can make a person do wrong. We hold that power. It's just a question of how far we're willing to take it.

"If they can force you," Seneca has Hercules say in one of his plays, "then you've forgotten how to die."

Remember that.

Fortune Favors the Bold

~

It is one of the oldest and most universal proverbs of the ancient world: *audentis Fortuna iuvat* in the *Aeneid*; *fortis Fortuna adiuvat* in one of Terence's plays; ʽτοῖς τολμῶσιν ἡ τύχη ξύμφορος from Thucydides. To Pliny, the Roman admiral and author, *Fortes fortuna iuvat*.

Fortune favors the bold. Fortune favors the brave.

It favors the big plans. It favors the risk-taking.

The decision to lead the charge. The decision to break ranks. The decision to try something new. The decision to accept the crazy challenge. To ask them to marry you, to take that trip, to raise your hand, to throw that long ball because with the game on the line you're no longer worried about interceptions. While the odds are often against these choices, know that the momentum of history is secretly with you. The crowd is with you, ready to cheer when you win. The more you put yourself out there, the more luck seems to come your way.

The architect Daniel Burnham is said to have advised his students to *make no little plans*. He was telling them to think big.

To tackle big problems. Not to get stuck on the onesie-twosies of life, but to try to *reach*. To do something so new and different that it scared them.

All the great commanders and entrepreneurs of history were successful because of the risks they took. Because while they may have been scared, they weren't afraid. Because they *dared greatly*. They entered the arena. They rolled the dice. They had *guts*.

And more often than not, they got lucky. If they hadn't, we wouldn't be talking about them.

"It is my experience that bold decisions give the best promise of success," General Erwin Rommel would write in one of his letters. "But one must differentiate between strategic or tactical boldness and a military gamble. A bold operation is one in which success is not a certainty but which in case of failure leaves one with sufficient forces in hand to cope with whatever situation may arise. A gamble, on the other hand, is an operation which can lead either to victory or to the complete destruction of one's force. Situations can arise where even a gamble may be justified as, for instance, when in the normal course of events defeat is merely a matter of time, when the gaining of time is therefore pointless and the only chance lies in an operation of great risk."

It was Rommel's tactical and strategic boldness on the battlefield that made him such a wily opponent in North Africa at the beginning of World War II. Still, we cannot avoid condemning his lack of boldness against Hitler before the war broke out.

Indeed, it was a lack of courage by almost all the German generals, many of whom found Hitler deranged and repugnant but could not bring themselves to break military protocol and challenge him as he hijacked their country. These were some of the bravest men in the world, men who had faced fire and death many times, yet in conference meetings they fearfully fretted and hoped someone *else* would do something. Waiting, hoping, cowering, they were complicit in heinous crimes. We'll never fully understand their wrassling, but inaction sealed their fate.

In the end, all that was left to Rommel, having missed the moment where a little boldness would have gone a long way, was a gamble. But by 1944, the gamble was more justified. Defeat was merely a matter of time, so why not try? So he did. Fortune didn't quite favor the conspirators who tried to depose and kill Hitler in the July 20 plot, but history at least respects the attempt.

A little boldness now is worth a lot more than death-defying courage later. The former needs a lot less of fortune's favor to succeed than the latter.

Jeff Bezos, the founder of Amazon, has talked about how he doesn't do "bet the company bets." Because he doesn't have to—it's complacency that puts you in a position to have to take huge risks. It's the company that, after years of ignoring the trends, finally has to change or die. It's when you're making up for earlier deficiencies that you have to gamble everything.

Better, he says, to consistently make good bets every day. Calculated instead of careless. Incremental instead of incredibly dangerous.

Do the hard thing now.

Be steady and courageous today, in everything that counts.

You'll have to trust that it's not as risky as you think. That you are not as alone as you think.

There is something behind you on this, even if it doesn't feel that way. Fortune is here. Fate is smiling upon you. But she tires quickly. She will resent you if you make her wait.

Better risk now than gamble later.

In either case, boldly proceed.

The Courage to Commit

~

"The story of Theodore Roosevelt," the biographer Hermann Hagedorn wrote, "is the story of a small boy who read about great men and decided he wanted to be like them." You can detect just a hint of a sneer, can't you?

Roosevelt actually *believed*. In himself. In stories. In something larger than himself. Then and now, plenty of people found that absurd, even dangerous. It's even in the Bible. *When I became a man, I put away those childish thoughts.*

De Gaulle was similarly mocked. He honestly, earnestly believed in the *grandeur* of France. He thought there was such a thing as destiny. "France is a great power," he said, over and over again. A preposterous claim when she lay prostrate, at the mercy of the Allies on the one hand, in passive collaboration with the Nazis on the other.

You read some of his quotes and you wince. The cynical streak in us runs deep. We want people to grow up. Get real. Get over the fairy tales.

But without this belief, without the courage to go on despite the condescension, the criticism, the futility of it, where would we be? Certainly if de Gaulle had cared less about France, he'd have risked less to save it. It was his sincere, almost cringe-worthy faith in destiny that propelled him to create history. He willed himself into the role of a great man and reformed a great nation in the process. For Roosevelt, caring was a wellspring of courage. It's what motivated him to invite Booker T. Washington to the White House, despite the hesitation. It's why he charged up hills to face the enemy, why he refused to buckle under the pressure of corporate interests, and why he resisted the haughty superiority and indifference of his social class.

As General Mattis said, cynicism is cowardice. It takes courage to care. Only the brave believe, especially when everyone else is full of doubt.

They will laugh at you. Losers have always gotten together in little groups and talked about winners. The hopeless have always mocked the hopeful. The scared do their best to convince the brave there is no point in trying. Since the time of the Sophists, academics have, for whatever petty reason, used their considerable brains to muddy the waters rather than clear them.

This is the fog that the courageous have to cut through. The stony road we walk is not lined with cheerleaders but tempt-resses who want to lead us astray or convince us to quit. You're far more likely to have someone try to convince you that *this doesn't matter,* that *it won't make a difference,* than you are to be threatened or intimidated out of trying. It takes strength to stay pure, to keep caring, to be explicit and sincere about what polite company seems to believe is gauche.

It's why we don't even like to talk about courage, let alone virtue. It's old-fashioned. It's awkward. It's as cool as a motivational poster hung up over your bed. Better to play like you're better than that, lest you be judged for falling short.

But has anyone ever accomplished anything in a field they don't care about? Has anyone done the right thing ironically? Nobody became great without believing that such a thing was worth doing. Nobody is brave without first braving and triumphing over cynicism and indifference.

"Be not afraid of greatness," Shakespeare said. Let it enter your blood and spirit. Fight for it.

Who cares if they don't understand? Those who laugh at your charge up the mountain are those who can't even imagine taking the first step onto uncertain ground. You'll prove them wrong. And even if you don't, at least you were brave enough to go for it.

Nihilism is for losers.

Love Thy Neighbor

~

It is the touchstone of indifference and callousness. The story that proved something is deeply wrong with our modern world.

At 3 a.m. on March 13, 1964, a young woman named Kitty Genovese was brutally raped and stabbed outside her apartment building. As she cried for help, she was ignored. As the sounds of her murder reverberated through her neighborhood, more than three dozen people turned up their televisions, turned over in bed, or decided it didn't concern them.

Why? Fear. Selfishness. Alienation. Maybe they thought someone else would do something. Maybe they didn't believe they *could* do anything. The cowardice and indifference of the community allowed a serial rapist and murderer so much cover that he returned to steal fifty dollars from the victim's purse.

What would we have done if we had been in our apartment that night? Would a year of 636 murders and our own busy lives have numbed us to the screams of a dying woman?

Although the story has come to represent all the ills of today's society, in truth one of Kitty's neighbors was not so far gone as the others. Actually, more than one. One neighbor, hearing the sounds, called Sophia Farrar, herself a young woman in the building, to say they thought Kitty was in trouble.

Without a thought for her own safety, Sophia, in her thirties with a baby at home, dressed quickly and rushed to the sound. There Kitty lay in front of the door to the building, wedging it shut. Carefully opening the door, Sophia found Kitty barely alive, soaked in her own blood, stabbed through the chest and lungs. Whispering sweetly to Kitty, Sophia tried desperately to save her life. She shouted until someone called the paramedics. She encouraged her neighbor to hang on, that help was coming. She told the dying woman that she was loved, that someone was *there*.

It was too late. Kitty bled out in the ambulance on the way to the hospital.

"I only hope that she knew it was me," Sophia would say, "that she wasn't alone."

Yes, the story of Kitty Genovese is a story of cowardice and callousness, but it is also the story of a friend cradling another friend in her last moments, the comfort and the kindness that are still possible in a world that too many people have given up on.

What kind of friend and neighbor are you?

Kitty Genovese was a lesbian just beginning to live openly with her girlfriend—no minor statement in 1964. Yet she and

Sophia were friends who did more than say hello to each other in the hall. Kitty sometimes drove Sophia's son to school. Sophia would watch the couple's poodle when they went out of town. They were there for each other as neighbors must be. They helped each other as neighbors must do. When it counted, when tragedy befell Kitty, Sophia showed up.

"People glorify all sorts of bravery except the bravery they might show on behalf of their nearest neighbors," George Eliot observed in *Middlemarch*. Sophia Farrar is not the type of person we focus on. She was not mentioned in the famous *New York Times* story that brought the case to the attention of millions. She never gave interviews, never got any attention, never even defended herself against the implication that she was one of those thoughtless, cowardly neighbors.

But just because she was never credited, just because she didn't manage to save Kitty, doesn't take away from her courage. What matters is that Sophia tried to do something. She rushed to the scene, without a thought to her own safety. She called for help. She comforted. She *cared.* That's what heroes do.

We won't always be successful, but we have to try. We can't harden our hearts or turn up our televisions. We don't need to wait for some enormous moment. It's about what we do every day—for ourselves, for other people.

"I am proud to have decided right at the beginning," Varlam Shalamov explained about the test he experienced in that gulag, "that I would never be a foreman if my freedom could lead to another man's death, if my freedom had to serve the bosses by oppressing other people, prisoners like myself. Both my physical and spiritual strength turned out to be stronger than I thought in this great test and I am proud that I never sold anyone, never sent anyone to their death or to another sentence, and never denounced anyone."

The freedom of the modern world, the freedom of your success—this is not freedom not to care. It is not permission to be indifferent. Yes, you have a lot going on. Yes, most of the evil in the world is not your fault. Still, you don't get to close your ears to the screams of an innocent person downstairs.

Anne Frank's neighbor, a young woman named Miep Gies, about the same age as Sophia, for months had risked herself to protect and supply the Jewish family as they hid in the attic. We know how that story ended too—one neighbor betrayed them—but we have to focus on the people who strove valiantly to prevent that from happening. As Gies explains, we must have the courage to help, even if it's a hopeless battle. "Any attempt at action is better than inaction," she reflected years later. "An attempt can go wrong, but inaction inevitably results in failure."

We have to *try*. Because if we don't, who will?

We can't just bemoan the darkness of this world we live in. We have to search for the light. We have to *be* the light.

For our nearest neighbors. For one another.

Bold Is Not Rash

~

One man with courage can make a majority.

It's inspiring. It's also dangerous.

What if the man is wrong? Or an egomaniac? What if his cause is unjust? This is how despots are made and murderous regimes are built. This is how religious sects become doomsday cults.

One man can just as easily lead himself—and the majority—right off a cliff.

So it is important we understand that courage, as a virtue, must be weighed against the equally essential virtue of moderation. Indeed, Aristotle used courage to illustrate the concept of temperance. Courage, he said, was the midpoint between two vices—cowardice being the best known, but recklessness being equally dangerous.

It was said of the charge of the Light Brigade that Lord Lucan, who gave the order, was an overly cautious ass, while Lord Cardigan, who led the suicidal charge without question, was a reckless ass.* Both are bad, but we tend to chastise the former more than the latter.

This is a mistake. Fear can at least protect a person. Complete fearlessness is a recipe for ruin.

That's what Marcus Aurelius strove to be: "neither rash nor hesitant—nor bewildered nor at a loss . . . not obsequious—but not aggressive or paranoid either." The leader, just like the teenage boy who goes around picking fights, will eventually find themselves outmatched and they will lose—possibly more than just their pride. Worse, who knows who else may be dragged in and pay for their cockiness?

There is a story about a Spartan soldier recognized for his almost superhuman bravery in a war against Thebes. Yet after the battle, he was fined by the city's rulers for fighting without his armor—he was needlessly endangering a Spartan asset . . . himself.

Courage isn't about measuring dicks. Or idle bravado. It doesn't mean forsaking a motorcycle helmet because you think you're invincible. Courage is about risk, but only necessary risk. Only carefully considered risk.

This is why the truly brave are often rather quiet. No time for,

---

* Soldiers are expected to follow orders, but today they are also empowered, if they doubt the safety or morality of a command, to take it to their superior and up the "request mast" until the right thing is done.

no interest in, boasting. Besides, they know that bragging puts a target on their back, and what is to be gained from that? That doesn't mean they're timid or self-effacing. As Aristotle again points out, *straightforwardness* is the intermediate between exaggeration and belittling. When you know, *you know.*

When you encounter real courage in this world, you will feel its intensity before you see it. It will not manifest in a caricature of the thrill-seeker or the daredevil. The courageous do not, as we have said, run around half-cocked. They are not stupid and therefore do not actively seek conflict. Even in their daring, they will be subdued unless you happen to find them in the midst of one of those rare decisive moments where they must call upon their courage. And still, in action they will be deliberate and calm, methodical and measured.

To see courage embodied like this, it will look something like Stefan Zweig's picture of Magellan, the explorer whose courage was unquestionable:

> It is necessary here to insist once more that in Magellan audacity, boldness, invariably assumed a peculiar complexion. To act boldly did not, in his case, mean to act on the heat of impulse, but to lay his plans craftily, to do the dangerous thing with the utmost caution and after more careful consideration. His most venturesome schemes were, like good steel, forged in fire and then hardened in ice.

Our model is not the hot-headed but the cold-blooded. Grace under pressure is also expressed as *cool under pressure* for a reason. Caution and care are not antonyms for courage but complements.

Make sure you package them together.

We often have cause to regret our brashness.

But bravery?

Never.

Agency Is Taken, Not Given

~

It wasn't until April 2011, nearly four years after he had been attacked, four years of people constantly telling him there was *nothing you can do about it,* that Peter Thiel changed his mind.

Or rather, had his mind opened.

At a dinner in Berlin with a young man known only as Mr. A, Thiel had been discussing Gawker and the anguish it had caused him. He complained of the chilling effect the website had on the culture, the impunity with which it exposed people's private affairs, and the cruel glee it did it with. Mr. A, with no small amount of bravery himself, called out the billionaire to his face, suggesting that Peter use his now enormous resources to do something about it. *No,* Peter replied, parroting what he himself had been told so many times, *it just isn't possible.*

That's when he was hit with the words that each of us needs to hear: "What would the world look like if everyone thought that way?"

Although agency is something that every person is born with, few of us choose to assert it. We accept the limitations that other people put on us. We listen to what they tell us is feasible or not. We, upon reviewing the odds, make them an effective truth.

What fear does is deprive you of power by making you think you don't have any. If you don't believe you can do something, it's not only unlikely that you can do it, it's guaranteed that you won't even try. Which is why we need more people to break out of this mentality.

The pivotal moment for Florence Nightingale was the realization that she was never going to be given what she knew she needed. She discovered, as she wrote in her journal, that she'd need to *take* it. She had to demand the life she wanted.

"That is not French," Napoleon once replied to a person who told him a problem was impossible to solve. And then he went and *did* what others said could not be done, for himself, for France.

"It begins," Peter Thiel has written, "by rejecting the unjust tyranny of chance." He knew that, he just had to believe it.

Forget fatalism. Take control of your own life, as Nightingale did. Reject the pessimistic view that we are at the mercy of forces beyond our control. Yes, you *can* do something. You *must*.

If nobody believes in the great man of history theory, how will history be made? Who will make it?

Certainly not you. Certainly not the heroes we need.

Each one of us has within our hands the power to end our own captivity. Each one of us has the means to assert our agency. It begins with a choice, but it is ensured by action. Few men of accomplishment, da Vinci noted, got there by things happening to them. No, he said, *they* are what has happened.

So which will you be? The immovable object or the unstoppable force? The leader or the follower? The passive acceptance or the active resistance?

You have to believe you can make a difference. You have to *try* to make one. Because this too is an effective truth. The unreasonable person is the one who changes the world. The one who believes they can decide the end of the story, that's the one who at least has a chance of writing some history.

After that meeting in Berlin, Thiel would fund and oversee a conspiracy that shocked the world. Gawker was destroyed in a $140 million verdict for its egregious conduct in a totally unrelated case that Thiel slowly, steadily, stealthily brought to bear on them.*

You don't have to agree with Thiel's response. It's quite reasonable to be alarmed at the secret lawsuits he filed that eventually bankrupted the media company and quite nearly ended with him owning the site outright. In fact, you *should* question this. Because agency for its own sake matters very little—what matters are the ends to which we assert ourselves and our power.

But there is no disputing that what he pulled off was something few could have managed and all were afraid to try. He did

---

* A fuller version of his battle with Gawker is told in my book *Conspiracy*.

something no one thought was possible. He found agency where others saw nothing but impossibility. Instead of being someone whom events happened to, he made events. He did what *he* wanted, what *he* felt was necessary, what *he* felt made the world a freer, safer place.

When Violence Is the Answer

~

Shortly after his grand jury testimony against corrupt officers in the NYPD, Frank Serpico was reassigned to the Manhattan North precinct. As he showed up to work that first day, he could feel that something was wrong. Even though no one was looking at him, all the energy of the room was pointed in his direction.

It was a primal scene, one not unlike those played out on the savannah and the schoolyard for as long as such things have existed. An officer, no doubt selected for the assignment, quickly approached Serpico. Standing close to him, he removed a switchblade knife from his pocket that he held in his open hand. "We know how to handle guys like you," he said as his blade flashed out. "I ought to cut your tongue out."

But this officer did not understand that Serpico, like Frederick Douglass, was tired. He had had enough. In an instant, Serpico seized the man by the wrist, twisting it until he fell to the ground. Putting his knee on his back, Serpico pinned him to the ground and placed his 9mm semiautomatic against his skull.

"Move, you motherfucker," Serpico said, "and I'll blow your brains out."

There were fourteen rounds in the pistol. Enough for every single person in the room. Enough to make Serpico's point: He would not be intimidated. He would not be touched. He wasn't backing down.

Are these moments of ferocious intensity cool or impressive? No, it would be better if they never had to happen. No good guy should ever have to draw a gun on a bad guy. No one should ever have to defend themselves as a consequence of doing the right thing.

The world does not care about "should." Would you have preferred that Serpico had assented to corruption rather than defend himself? Should he have let himself be killed before he exposed it? Even Gandhi, a man of incredible gentleness and restraint, knew there was a line that must sometimes be crossed. "Where there is only a choice between cowardice and violence," he said, "I would advise violence."

They wanted to force Serpico not to talk. They wanted him to choose between his life and his cause. Instead, he turned the tables.

No one should seek out situations like these, but you should know that you may find yourself in one. And it will be then that you'll understand the truth of the expression popular with self-defense instructors: Violence is rarely the answer—but when it is, *it's the only answer.*

A Spartan general made the same point to some timid countrymen. Watching a mouse caught by a boy swing by its tail and bite its captor, the general said, "When the tiniest creature defends itself like this against aggressors, what ought men to do, do you reckon?"

As that mouse might attest, no species survives long without a will to protect itself. Without bravery, without the warrior ethos, no one—and no nation—survives long enough. There are plenty of brave pacifists out there, but even they understand at some level that their idealism is feasible only because others are willing to be pragmatic in their place.

Sometimes physical courage is required to protect moral courage. There will be moments when we are at risk—or someone we love is at risk. Kind words will not cut it. Poise will not protect us. What will be called for is intensity, aggression, a demonstration of force. In these moments, we cannot shy away. We cannot shrink.

We cannot be bullied. We cannot do nothing.

In those moments, we'll have to hit back, and we'll have to hit hard.

We must raise our fists. We must make our stand. Lest we end up on our knees.

To Get Up and Leave

~

Here's a short summary of the journey to America of Maria Giovanna, the mother of Frank Serpico. She and her husband, hoping for better opportunities, made plans to emigrate from Italy. She was designated to go first, and so she did, just twenty-seven years old, traveling by sea, seven months pregnant.

During the crossing, she went into labor and gave birth prematurely on the ship. She arrived in a new land in the dead of winter, hemorrhaging from childbirth, knowing no English. The relative who was supposed to meet her never arrived. In the days before neonatal care, she would lose her precious baby and end up in a charity hospital. Alone.

A week later, she was rescued by distant family members, whom she lived with in Brooklyn *for a year,* supporting herself doing backbreaking factory work—quietly, *stoically*—while she waited for her husband to come over from Italy.

When Serpico's father did arrive, the only work he could find was shining shoes. It would be almost a decade before he could open his own shop, as a cobbler, which had been his dream from the beginning. But in time he would raise three children, one of whom would go on to defy and reform the NYPD almost single-handedly.

To leave your home, to leave what you know, to risk it all for the hope—usually a dismal, naïve, projected hope—for a better life? To cross oceans and deserts, to brave gunfire, prejudice, walls, and uncertainty? It may well be the most courageous thing a human being can do.

It is a beautiful, inspiring thing.

Goebbels would refer to the refugees and emigrants of Europe as "cadavers on leave." Just bodies, fleeing, somebody else's problem, soon to be dead somewhere else. *They're not sending their best.*

The boldness, the gamble, the sheer tenacity and determination? They might not be the most educated, they might not be the most wealthy, some of them might well be leaving mistakes and failures behind them, but immigrants are by definition exhibiting a virtue we all admire. Tired? Meek? These are indefatigable warriors. They are the descendants of pioneers and explorers. Where would we be without this kind of courage?

Who would *not* want it infused into their economy and culture? Who can't learn something from this in our own cushier, safer lives?

And of course, emigration is not the only form of getting up and leaving. Sometimes it's the courage to quit a job that's become a dead end. Sometimes it's calling it on a project that we've sunk our whole life and life's savings into. Or it's walking away from a political party. It's deciding to divorce after many unhappy years together.

We did our best. We struggled. We fought, bravely, intensely. It didn't work.

Some people use the fact that things are bad as an excuse. Some people use their surroundings as a reason to despair. Some people think a lack of opportunity is a problem that resolves itself. Other people get up and do something about it.

Which one are you?

In his dialogue with Laches, Socrates asks for a definition of courage. The answer he gets is a good one: "Courage is a sort of endurance of the soul." Socrates can't leave it at that, of course, because enduring in the wrong thing, staying and continuing in a foolhardy or impossible endeavor, can hardly be described as wise.

Leaving is scary. The end of something can feel like a kind of dying. Somewhere or something new means uncertainty. It is risky. It is painful. It requires hard decisions. No one can promise you that the next place, the next try will go better. But it's pretty certain that continuing to do the same thing in the same way in the same place over and over is not just insanity, but eventually a form of cowardice.

It doesn't matter if somebody is from Mexico or Syria or Sri Lanka, or if they're walking away from the wreckage of a failed business or a successful niche that got stale. It doesn't matter if every letter of the law was followed, if they were perfect angels—what counts is that they're doing something. They are controlling what happens to them, not the other way around. They are making a big bet. One that takes real cojones.

Knowing what it takes to leap ourselves, we ought to admire it when we see it in others. We should let it inspire us too—no situation is hopeless, we're never without agency. We can always bravely pack up and move.

Do Your Job

At a quarter to twelve on October 21, 1805, Horatio Nelson ordered his flagman to signal to the fleet at the opening of the Battle of Trafalgar: "England expects every man will do his duty."

He wanted them to fight. Up close. To do the jobs they'd been trained to do.

Fear gives us no shortage of reasons why we can't do any or all of those things: It's too hard. It's too dangerous. The odds are too high. The orders don't make sense. The leader should have put me in charge.

Courage cuts through the noise. It reminds you what the situation calls for. It reminds you what you signed up for.

We all have different duties. There is the duty of a doctor or an officer of the court. There is the duty of a soldier. The duty of a parent to a child, a spouse to a partner. There is also the duty of any person with potential, the duty of any citizen with a conscience. Duty is not just doing what you swore in your oath, or *not* doing what is proscribed by law, it is what is demanded of us as decent human beings. Our duty is to do the right thing—right now.

Not halfheartedly either. But with all the earnestness and commitment that we've got. With the belief that we can make a difference. That we must.

It will be hard. The oath of your office may put you in an impossible position. You can find yourself like Helvidius, commanded by the emperor to stand down, forbidden by duty and self-respect to obey. There will be a tension between interests. There will be criticism and risk.

But?

And?

Do you know what happens when we avoid the hard things? When we tell ourselves it doesn't matter? When someone fails to do their job in the moment, or kicks a tough decision upstairs or down the road? It forces someone else to do it later, at even greater cost. The history of appeasement and procrastination show us: The bill comes due eventually, with interest attached.

The thing about duty is that we have a choice not to do it, of course, but at the same time, we know that really, there is no choice. Or rather, there is only *one* choice.

For five and a half hours, the British fleet would clash with the French and Spanish in the Battle of Trafalgar. It was the high-water mark of Napoleon's plan to conquer Europe. It was one of the hardest-fought naval battles in history.

Nelson could have watched it from a place of safety, and,

having already lost an arm in a previous battle, that might have been the prudent thing. But too much was on the line to lead from a distance. Besides, a commander must brave the same risks they ask their soldiers to take. So he paced the deck of his ship, impervious to the dangers, dictating orders and making adjustments. He threw everything he had at the enemy, poured every bit of himself into the moment.

Then a bullet pierced Nelson's spine.

Carried belowdecks, he would utter his last words: "Thank God I have done my duty."

We should all be proud to go out with such a thought. "Any dangerous spot is tenable if brave men will make it so," John F. Kennedy said.

It's *made* so by those who do their job. Who answer the call. Serpico facing down his fellow officers. Nightingale challenging the bureaucracy and apathy of her time. Roosevelt kicking a hornet's nest with Booker T. Washington.

Churchill, holding that fire, drawing in allies, refusing to surrender, so he could save Britain. Like Nelson, he believed there was "something going on in space and time and beyond space and time, which whether we like it or not, spells duty."

It called. He answered. So many have answered. Will you?

You Can Beat the Odds

~

It was a fix of his own making, but that didn't make it any less of a fix.

The North Koreans had invaded the South and quickly overrun the ROK forces. General Douglas MacArthur, the theater commander, had been caught off guard in Japan. Backed by the UN, he flooded South Korea with troops, but it was barely enough to hold on.

Seoul fell. The noose tightened. The American troops, trapped in what was called the Pusan Perimeter, were given the order to "stand or die."

The hope of victory was dim; dim in everyone except MacArthur.

He had an idea: Mount an amphibious invasion at the port of Inchon, some 150 miles up the South Korean coast, landing *behind* the invaders. Catching the enemy by surprise, he believed, could turn the tide of the war.

But the tide was part of the problem. If you were designing a port to make an invasion impossible, it would be hard to do better than dreary, industrial Inchon. It had every geographic handicap you could imagine. Mud flats. Rocky shores. Surrounded by concrete seawalls and piers, this beachless port was a potential killing field at low tide, a treacherous rip current of watery graves in high tide. It was accessible just *two days* a month. And even then, for but a few hours . . . if it wasn't already blocked by mines.

Everyone had reservations.

Except MacArthur, who, striding to a blackboard, wrote in French, *"De Qui Objet?"*—What is the object? It was to surprise the enemy. To put pressure on them. He circled the port on the map. "That's where we should land, Inchon—go for the throat." They shouldn't take "counsel of their fears," he said—it was a matter of willpower and courage.

His superiors reviewed the operation. They were not impressed. "The operation is not impossible," the vice admiral of the Navy told MacArthur, "but I do not recommend it."

This should have been discouraging. Instead, it actually excited MacArthur. They were telling him *there was a chance.* That's what "not impossible" means. Whether it's a 1 percent chance or .0001 percent, all that courage needs to hear is that there is a possibility.

It's hard? Unlikely? No matter.

As it happens, the sheer improbability was why MacArthur liked his chances. "The North Koreans would regard an Inchon landing as impossible," he said. "I could take them by surprise."

High, but not insuperable, hurdles are the perfect opportunity for the brave to win stunning victories.

No committee coming from the safety of Washington to point out the "realities" of a situation was going to convince MacArthur. He had remembered his father's words: "Doug, councils of war breed timidity and defeatism." His own estimate of the odds was one in five thousand.

That was enough. "I can almost hear the ticking of the second hand of destiny," he said. "We must act now or we will die . . . Inchon will succeed. And it will save a hundred thousand lives."

On September 15, 1950, the guns opened up the invasion. With just minutes to spare, some thirteen thousand Marines landed. When MacArthur came ashore, the first thing he did was throw up. But he'd done it. He had beaten the odds. Fortune favored the bold.*

Where would we be without people brave enough to challenge the odds? If every entrepreneur, activist, and general listened to the predictions, what kind of world would this be? If every oncologist faced the facts of their diagnoses, no patient would ever be saved. If every team down in the fourth quarter believed they were beaten, there would never be any comebacks.

---

* It's worth noting that six months later MacArthur would be unceremoniously fired from his job because the success had gone to his head. Remember: Boldness is not rashness. It can't be when you're gambling with other people's lives.

If every RAF pilot had looked at the numbers in 1940—a one-in-ten chance of dying in each sortie—would Britain have been able to hold out?

If we only did what we were sure of, if we only proceeded when things were favorable, then history would never be made. The averages have been against everything that ever happened—that's why we call it *the mean*.

We have to remember that these polls, these estimations, these statistical models—these things are static. What they cannot predict for, what they cannot account for, is the individual with agency, the human being who makes events happen rather than simply sitting back and waiting for things to happen to them.

It takes courage to look at the averages and say, "I am not average." To say, "Somebody will be the exception and it may as well be me."

That's what courage is. In fact, there is no courage without bad odds, without a willingness to risk losing—the job, the game, the deal, your life. If it was a sure thing, what would be brave about it?

You have to realize that you are not average. You never have been. You are one of one. You have always had what it took to defy the odds.

If you don't believe that, might you be reminded that your *very existence* is perhaps the least likely thing to ever happen? The odds of you being born, some scientists have estimated, are in the realm of one in four hundred trillion—but in truth this understates it. Consider everything that had to happen for your parents to meet, for you to survive, for you to find yourself here at this moment, thinking about what you may embark on. You are more than a miracle, you are a miracle on the spectrum of unlikely miracles. Yet here you are.

You're going to let the fact that unhindered success is rare deter you? You're going to let *the mean* tell you what you can and can't do? You're going to let them wear you down and convince you to play it safe? Or not at all? That's not a recipe for living, for greatness, for *goodness*.

Of course, you can't just disregard dangers because they are inconvenient—especially when other people depend on you. As we've said, the entrepreneur constantly taking those "bet the company bets" we talked about will eventually go bust. He or she may walk away to gamble again, but the employees will take the hit.

Still, there is no escaping: Sometimes we must be brave enough to defy the odds, but we do this only when there is a *real chance* of success. And we do it rarely, when we have no other choice.

Make Them Proud

~

The last word of Marcus Porcius Cato as he bravely faced death on the battlefield was the name of his father.

The last words of Porcia, Cato's daughter, dying as a result of her role in conspiring against Caesar? "I am Cato's daughter."

Their father had set an example. They would not let him down. They would go down fighting.

While few of us are heirs to such a famous bloodline as the children of the powerfully determined and incorruptible Cato the Younger, we are nonetheless descendants of a long and illustrious tradition. We are, indirectly, the heir to Cato and to all heroes who have ever lived, because we wouldn't be here without them.

So how could we possibly justify letting them down?

As Longfellow wrote:

Lives of great men all remind us
We can make our lives sublime,

And, departing, leave behind us
Footprints on the sands of time.

Here, in the middle of this difficult time—personally, professionally, politically—we can find strength in the examples of the past. We can let great deeds and inspiring words steel our resolve and harden our commitment.

When Apple had drifted from its innovative and rebellious roots, this was a tactic Steve Jobs used to bring the company back on track. "One way to remember who you are," he said, "is to remember who your heroes are."

Maybe for you that's Jesus, refusing to flee, going bravely to the cross. Maybe it's Audie Murphy—the most decorated soldier in American history—climbing into that burning tank destroyer and using its .50 caliber machine gun for over an hour, keeping the enemy at bay, even after he was wounded, refusing to give an inch of ground, holding the woods until reinforcements came. Maybe it's Muhammad Ali, risking it all to protest the war in Vietnam. Maybe it's Florence Nightingale pushing past her parents, past the constraints of her time, to herald a new world.

Harry Burns didn't want to ruin his political career, because his widowed mother depended on him for support. Yet ultimately his mother was not a liability—she was an inspiration. He did the right thing *for* her, even if there was some risk to her. And the same must be true for our families. We step forward, we step up because we want to make them proud. Because we would not betray them.

Most of our brave ancestors and predecessors are gone now, and yet does their example not return to us? Does their memory not float above us, to be reached for whenever needed?

We must turn to them in our darkest moments. This is ready-made courage we can draw on, whenever we feel ourselves wavering. Think of those who led brave lives before you, think of your connection to them.

"You had a brave man for a grandfather," Seneca's father wrote, hoping to inspire his own children and their children. "See to it that you are braver."

Imagine that your own ancestors—of blood and of bravery—are standing here, watching you, protecting you. Remind yourself *what they would do right here and right now.* You can't let them down.

So be braver. Right now. Here, in this decisive moment.

When We Rise Above Ourselves . . .

> Man is pushed by drives. But he is pulled by values.
>
> VIKTOR FRANKL

If there is a certain unreasonableness to courage, there is something even harder to explain. Altruism. Selflessness. Indeed, evolutionary psychologists, biologists, and dramatists alike have struggled to make sense of it for years.

"Human folly," the historian T. R. Fehrenbach observed, "is easier to explain than human valor."

Courage has clear rewards. One takes a risk because they hope for a payoff—something others are afraid to reach for. But what about sacrificing oneself? Or sacrificing deeply *for* something? There's courage and then there is *heroism,* the highest form of courage. The kind embodied in those who are willing to give, perhaps give *everything,* for someone else.

There was once a particularly craven leader who stood in a

military cemetery and looked out over the graves of those who had been lost in the nation's wars over the centuries. "I don't get it," he said. "What was in it for them?" When most people ask that question, it's out of a kind of humility and awe, a desire to understand an incredible phenomenon. But for the transactional, the cowardly, and the selfish, the bafflement is sincere. Why would anyone give up their life for someone else? What kind of deal is that?

The logic of self-preservation is strong. Especially in those of us with pragmatic streaks. It takes a stronger person to override it. A strange paradox: Those without a strong sense of self are unlikely to be brave, yet the highest form of bravery demands a kind of selflessness that is, in some cases, suicidal. How does that work? Perhaps it can't be explained in words. Perhaps it is beyond our limits of understanding outside the moment in which it occurs—like those feats of superhuman *physical* strength where mothers lift cars off small children.

Yet we know how essential this is to our survival as a species, let alone as the good guys. There's a reason that our greatest art celebrates it, that the names of these heroes remain touchstones centuries after their deeds.

Courage is rare enough, but heroism is that rarer form of courage, the one that is so powerful we have trouble staring it directly in the face. You hear it in Medal of Honor acceptance speeches from soldiers, or the interview with the hero who just dove in front of a train to save somebody: "I just did what anyone would have done." If that were actually true, we wouldn't be making such a big deal of it.

True heroism shames us. Humbles us. It moves us beyond reason—because it came from something beyond reason. Which is why we worship it so.

It's self-evident why the survival rate of those who manage to touch this greatness is not high. But then again, that is the beauty of it—in some cases, they died so that we could live. We fail them and we fail ourselves if we don't wrestle with the meaning of this sacrifice.

PART III
THE
HEROIC

In the world's broad field of battle,
In the bivouac of Life,
Be not like dumb, driven cattle!
Be a hero in the strife!

—HENRY WADSWORTH LONGFELLOW

If courage—moral and physical—is the act of putting your ass on the line, then the definition of the heroic is very simple: It is risking oneself *for* someone else. It's putting it on the line not just for your own benefit but for the benefit of someone, something, some larger cause. Is this not one of the greatest expressions of the human species? In those situations where real danger lurks, where hope has disappeared, nobody cries for a manager. Nobody cries for the calculated reasoning of a logician. They cry for action, for a hero—for someone to save them, to step up and do what we cannot do for ourselves. And in answering this call, the hero enters, however briefly, a higher plane. They touch the face of the gods. *Megalopsuchia*. The Stoics called it "greatness of soul." Courage *plus,* we might call it. De Gaulle was once asked what he meant when he spoke of France's "grandeur." He answered: "The road one takes to surpass oneself." This, this is the bravery that we hold up above the others. Because it is so rare, so much more profound, something we see only fleetingly. To get there, we must triumph over fear, we must cultivate courage in daily life, and we must be ready to seize the opportunities life presents us—however big or small. Our need for heroes is great. Will you be one?

Going Beyond the Call . . .

T he Greeks were not perfect. The Spartans least of all.
But they were not bootlickers and they were better than
the tyrannical, insatiable king who bore down on them in 480 BC.

Xerxes, the ruler of the enormous Persian empire, sought sub-
jugation and revenge. The Greeks had offended him—rebuffing
his emissaries with insolence and foiling his father's invasion a
decade before—and now, with an enormous army, he marched
into Greece.

Some Greek city-states saw the writing on the wall and
surrendered. Some took large bribes to switch sides. The already shaky confederacy of Greek nations—from Sparta to
Athens, Thebes, Argos, and Corinth—stood on the precipice of
collapse, and with it rested the entire future of Western civilization, though they could not have fully known this in the moment. Would Xerxes conquer the West? Would an all-powerful
king, worshipped as a god, stamp out the embers of freedom and
equality, extinguishing a way of life we are fortunate enough to
enjoy today?

As the allies struggled to come together, struggled to prepare, it was decided: A small army, led by three hundred Spartans and their ruler, Leonidas, would rush to Thermopylae, the "Hot Gates," to hold back the Persians as long as they could. If they could make a strong stand, perhaps Greece could be inspired to fight on.

"They say that the barbarian has come near and is coming on while we are wasting time," Leonidas told his soldiers. "Truth, soon we shall either kill the barbarians, or else we are bound to be killed ourselves." And so they marched, three hundred of Sparta's most elite soldiers—to a man, each one the father of at least one living son—traversing some 250 miles to face perhaps the worst odds in the history of warfare. They picked up some reinforcements from a few neighboring states, but it is believed that between five thousand and seven thousand Greeks eventually stood against a Persian force that some ancient historians have claimed numbered as many as *one million* men.

Their only advantage? Thermopylae, a narrow coastal passage near the Aegean Sea, which would neutralize Xerxes's overwhelming strength. Also, unlike their invader, the Spartans were actually fighting *for* something: They were prepared to fight—and die—so that others might stay free.

"If you had any knowledge of the noble things of life," Leonidas told Xerxes, "you would refrain from coveting others' possessions; but for me to die for Greece is better than to be the sole ruler over the people of my race."

Of course, the insatiable conquerors of history have no understanding of such things. The very first thing Xerxes did was try to bribe the Spartans. It had worked on some of the weaker city-states, and it was certainly the kind of temptation that Xerxes would have lunged at had he been in the same position.

Not Leonidas. Not for a descendent of Hercules. To take the easy choice? To betray others for your own gain? To advance one's position but do it through treachery? "The Greeks have learned from their fathers to gain lands, not by cowardice but by valor," Leonidas replied.

He chose virtue. He chose courage.

This idea of valor—not just courage but a commitment to something larger than themselves—was what convinced the Greeks this mission was even worth attempting. How could you possibly risk so few against that many? one ally asked Leonidas. "If you men think that I rely on numbers," he replied, "then all Greece is not sufficient, for it is but a small fraction of their numbers; but if on men's valor, then this number will do." And so when Xerxes asked the Spartans to surrender their arms, the laconic reply was: "Come and take them."

For four days, just the threat of tangling with the Spartans kept the Persians at bay. Sometime on August 18, the assault began. Line after line of Persian soldiers was thrown against the phalanx of Greeks. There they clashed among the rocks, the Spartans fighting in lockstep, not just for their country, but as true heroes always do, for the man next to them.

Toward the end of the first day, Xerxes ordered his most fearsome soldiers, the Ten Thousand Immortals, into the breach. A Spartan remarked to Leonidas that the Immortals were near. Leonidas reassured him, "Yes, and we are also near to them." To Xerxes's horror, rising three times in anguished impotence, even these troops were hurled back at great loss.

As the first day bled into the second, Leonidas was not fooled by the victories he had won. He had always known, regardless of the hope of reinforcements, that this was a one-way mission. Yet he had come all the same. He was fighting for time. He was there to prove a point as well: His act of *devotio* was meant to call to the courage of the Greeks who wavered on whether to surrender or resist. They fought on, the second day as brutal as the first.

By the third day, it was clear that the Persians had found a way to attack from the rear. A warning came about the enemy's strength: Xerxes's archers would fire enough arrows to block out the sun. "Then we shall fight in the shade," Leonidas said. Then he ordered his men to dine well, because they were most likely to dine next in the afterworld. He attempted to select three injured men to return to Sparta with news, hoping secretly to spare their lives as well. To a man, they rejected this golden ticket: "I came with the army, not to carry messages, but to fight," the first replied. The next: "I should be a better man if I stayed here." The third: "I will not be behind these, but first in the fight."

With nothing left to say, the Spartans stood in silence. Who among them was not bearing wounds from the previous day's fighting? Who was not exhausted? Who was not thinking of their children? Of the country they had left behind?

By nine o'clock, the sun was up and the heat with it. They sweated in their armor. Their bodies coursed with whatever reserves of adrenaline and patriotism remained. They would never see Sparta or their families again.

Leonidas gave the order to *march forward*. They stepped outside the protection of the rocky gates to meet the enemy in the open, inflicting extra damage as they took their final stand. The Persians hit them with a fury, whipped from behind by their slave drivers, backed by so many soldiers that they could afford to trample wounded or fallen comrades as the endless waves of men followed, one after another.

The Spartans dispatched them methodically, as fiercely as before, at times even feigning to have broken ranks, letting the Persians rush forward, and then reforming to slaughter them. Each time a cry of exhilaration would go up. For this brief moment, uncommon valor was a common virtue. The men passed beyond themselves, fighting and performing with an almost otherworldly excellence. But the Spartans knew, *they knew*. This was it.

They would not grow old. To a man they would fall. And soon.

Leonidas was killed in the middle of the final day, fulfilling a prophecy he had long believed, that a Spartan king would have to die lest Greece be destroyed by an invader. His men rushed out, in one, two, three attempts to retrieve his body. On the fourth, they managed. Then right back to the fight.

Their spears broke off from use. No reinforcements came. Now the word spread through the ranks—it was time. They retreated back to the gates. Here, they fought with only their swords, and upon losing these, they resorted to their hands and teeth.

Eventually, inevitably, they were overwhelmed. It had been three days of battle, plus the four before. They bought their country one week. It cost Xerxes countless men, but mostly time he did not have. More, it shook his confidence. How many more Spartans are there in Greece? he asked one of his advisers. Do they all fight like this? *There are thousands more,* came the reply, *none are equal to these fallen men, but all are just as good at fighting.*

Greece also understood what was at stake. No one could deny the gesture the Spartans had made. No one could deny the call to do their part.

Centuries later, Churchill remarked of the RAF's incredible defense of Britain during the Battle of Britain that "never before have so many owed so much to so few." This was not quite true, for even the stand of those few owes a debt first to the three hundred Spartans. It's not a stretch to argue that *all* the accomplishments of Western civilization, from the Renaissance to the American Revolution, would not have happened were it not for the sacrifice at Thermopylae.

And so those three hundred soldiers who sacrificed, as the soldiers at Gettysburg did, as the RAF did, became more than men. They became almost like gods.

It is almost offensively clichéd now to use the phrase "Freedom isn't free." Nonetheless, it is true. Purchased there in the glorious defeat at Thermopylae were the victories that the Greeks were able to achieve at Salamis and Plataea. The Magna Carta, the Declaration of Independence, the United Nations— all of it rooted there in the fight at the Hot Gates. The freedom that everyone loves but so many tend to abuse? It was won there too, by those fathers who fought side by side, knowing for certain they would not live to see the fruits of their labor, just as the tree you sit under was planted long ago by a man or a woman who cared about the future.

Theirs was not to reason why. Theirs was to do and to die. As the ancient inscription at the battlefield reads, "Tell the Spartans passerby, here obedient to her laws we lie." Their example of courage and selflessness stands eternal. None of them survived, yet they turned out to be far more immortal than the Persian troops who killed them.

Gates of Fire, the epic historical novel of this battle by Steven Pressfield, is today passed from soldier to soldier, person to person, as a kind of tribute to that example. The central question of the book was: *What is the opposite of fear?* It's not enough to simply conquer or quench fear. In writing the book, Pressfield wanted to know, as the Spartans did, what lay beyond it. If fear was the vice, what was the virtue? It's not just courage. Because you can be courageous for selfish reasons. You have to override fear to jump out of an airplane, sure, but if you're doing it for fun, is it really that meaningful?

It wasn't just the men and their arms that made feats at Thermopylae possible. It was also the wives who not only allowed their husbands to go, but whose courage and iron self-discipline was the backbone of the country. The toughness and selflessness of Spartan women is legendary. When one Spartan king was killed in a vicious coup, his mother rushed to his body, and when the killers offered to spare her if she kept quiet, she stood up and defied them. Her last words, as she offered her neck: "May this only be of service to Sparta."

We are mistaken to see the Spartans as mere warriors, just courageous fighters. As Pressfield concludes, the opposite of fear—the true virtue contrasted with that vice—was not fearlessness. *The opposite of fear is love.* Love for one another. Love for ideas. Love for your country. Love for the vulnerable and the weak. Love for the next generation. Love for *all*. Is that not what hits us in the solar plexus when we hear Leonidas's final, tearful words to his wife before he leaves? "Marry a good man who will treat you well, bear him children, and live a good life."

And it is this profound, marrow-deep love that allows one to rise above the logic of self-preservation and achieve true greatness, whether that's shielding someone from a bullet, risking your job to speak out in defense of the common good, or fighting—against all hope—for a cause you know is right.

Florence Nightingale cared tenderly for the suffering of the sick in her country. De Gaulle fought, exasperatingly hard, to preserve France. The Spartans, at the Hot Gates, were something beyond this, truly selfless, giving the most a person can possibly give. Sure, not all selflessness requires the ultimate sacrifice, but there is no selflessness *without* sacrifice. The sacrifice they made was incredible—all the more so because it had not been for themselves or their own people that they made it. Leonidas could have survived, if he chose. He and the Spartans could have ruled all of Greece. Nevertheless, he went and died so that all those Greeks could be free. So that *we* could be free.

If courage is rare, then this kind of heroism is a critically endangered species. If courage by itself is unreasonable, then love in this higher form—the truly selfless kind—is insane. It is baffling in its majesty. It is real human greatness. It is us transcending logic, self-interest, and millions of years of our own biology to find quarter, however briefly, in a higher realm.

The Spartans are the heroes we recognize as the embodiment of that idea, but we should remember that they are standins. They represent the anonymous courage of countless resisters for all time, for people who testified in trials and faced reprisals, people who registered to vote and were beaten for it, union organizers who went up against robber barons, pioneers who set out rescue parties, athletes who played through career-ending injuries to keep their team in the game or their families fed. These were selfless moments of *megalopsuchia*.

What we're willing to give—that full measure of our devotion, to the effort, to a stranger, to what must be done—that's what takes us higher. That's what transforms us from brave to *heroic*. Maybe for a moment, maybe to just one person, maybe to be enshrined in the history books for all time.

The Cause Makes All

A s Gawker stifled under the slow, unrelenting secret pressure from Peter Thiel, its editors grew desperate. They needed to generate more traffic. They wanted to prove their transgressive bona fides. Maybe they could sense the times were changing, and yet, having still never been held accountable, they believed they were invincible.

In July 2015, the flashpoint came. The site published a story outing a gay media executive with two children who was being shaken down by a male escort. It was one of those mean but titillating stories they'd rushed to print so many times in the past, the kind everyone else was afraid to touch. But now something was different—the financial and public relations realities forced Gawker's owner to pull the story. He tried to explain to the staff just how far they had drifted from what the public would accept, and what he was willing to accept as a gay man himself.

Objecting to any interference from management, the site's two editors resigned in rebellion. They would *not* be second-guessed by corporate. They would *not* censor themselves. They would pay with their jobs to insist on it.

We can grant that it takes courage to quit on principle, to blow up your career over a story. It's also obvious to any person with a moral compass that this was the wrong hill to die on. It was a hill they shouldn't have even been on in the first place.

Of course, the truly courageous thing would have been to look in the mirror and reckon with what they had done. But they couldn't. So they doubled down and gambled their jobs on it.

There was bravery in this, but as a French general watching the Light Brigade march unthinkingly, needlessly toward death said, *C'est magnifique . . . c'est de la folie*—It is magnificent . . . it is madness. The whole thing was madness, in fact. Who even remembers what the Crimean War was about? Nobody then really knew either.

Editorial independence is important. But to do what? For what *reason*?

The Gawker editors couldn't have told you.

There were many brave soldiers in the Confederacy. Same goes for the British army in its wars in India and Africa. Or Japan as it defended the islands it had taken in the Pacific.

You read about some of these feats and your jaw drops.

Yet, intuitively, you know that there is something empty about this courage. It's empty because of how craven and wrong what they fought for was.

As the poet Lord Byron said:

> 'Tis the Cause makes all,
> Degrades or hallows courage in its fall.

Courage is not an independent good. Heroes have a *reason*. What good is a deed if done for its own sake? What weight does bravery have as a parlor trick or as an exercise of vanity? Or of unquestioning obedience? What if it's done for the wrong thing?

John F. Kennedy in his book *Profiles in Courage* highlights the political stand of Edmund G. Ross, who bucked his party and voted against the impeachment of Andrew Johnson. Of all the chapters of that book, it has aged the worst. It's always difficult to stand alone, but in this case, Ross was standing for the preservation of *literal* white supremacy. Worse, by resisting a controversial change at the time—the first impeachment of a sitting president—Ross helped set a precedent that has since made it insanely difficult to remove bad presidents from office.

The CEO who stares down incredible odds to further an exploitative, toxic business. The anti-vaxxer risking opprobrium and illness, literally going against the herd. The dictator who seizes power in a dazzling, daring coup. The police who resign in solidarity when an officer is punished for pushing over an old man in Buffalo. The soldiers taken into custody for refusing to testify against Second Lieutenant William Calley after My Lai.

Courage. Hollow courage.

As an instructor at the U.S. Naval Academy explained: Jumping on a grenade only matters if you jump on a grenade *to accomplish something,* to save someone. The difference between raw courage and the heroic lies in the *who.* Who was it for? Was it truly selfless? Was it for the greater good? There is a logic to heroism, even as illogical as it is to override your own self-preservation.

"The Stoics," Cicero would write, "correctly define courage as the virtue which champions the cause of right . . . No one has attained true glory who has gained a reputation for courage by treachery and cunning."

It's good to be brave. The world does want to know if you have cojones.

But the why, the where, the when of it counts.

The cause makes all.

The Braver Thing Is Not to Fight

~

Lincoln won the Civil War.

What he doesn't get enough credit for are his efforts to prevent the whole thing in the first place.*

Despite his fair victory in a democratic election, despite repeated assurances that he had no intention of exceeding his constitutional authority, the South seceded—before he had even taken the oath of office.

Yet what did he conclude his first inaugural address with? A call to the better angels of everyone's nature. "We are not enemies, but friends," he said passionately. "We must not be enemies. Though passion may have strained, it must not break our bonds of affection."

And when the South began to besiege federal forts and stockades, Lincoln maintained this line. He would not rise to

---

* Also worth crediting Prince Albert of England, who in the final days of his life kept Britain out of the U.S. Civil War (which quite easily could have become a world war).

anger. He would not be provoked. Even at the showdown over Fort Sumter in South Carolina, Lincoln chose only to send much-needed food and supplies to the trapped men, not guns or troops, because he would not unnecessarily escalate an unbelievably tense situation.

A confrontation that doesn't need to happen, shouldn't happen. Suffering, discomfort, worry—these things take courage to endure. But wisdom and compassion obligate us not just to avoid them when unnecessary but to try to protect others from them too. That's why heroes fight just as hard to prevent a conflict as they do inside the rare conflict they find themselves in.

Gandhi had said he'd rather choose violence than cowardice. What he and other nonviolence practitioners chose instead was something even more magnificent and heroic. It took even more courage to do battle without weapons, to fight with one's soul and one's spirit against armed and angry enemies. Imagine the courage of young Malala Yousafzai, targeted and left for dead by the Taliban, for trying to go to school. "Even if there was a gun in my hand and he was standing in front of me," she said, "I would not shoot him."

Is that not tougher than the toughest warrior?

The problem is that usually this kind of heroism is less cinematic than a cavalry charge. People want to read books about wars . . . not the diplomacy that prevented them from happening. People want to hear about the whistleblowers . . . not the leaders who were able to effectively reform companies from the inside without it needing to come to that. We make movies about those brave iconoclasts who do everything differently . . . but what about someone who makes a difference *and* is able to fit in and function in society?

Remember: Nobody gets credit for things that didn't happen. We think about FDR and how he stared down the Great Depression. His real accomplishments were the reforms that prevented countless other future depressions, that were responsible for catching financial crooks and manipulations, reforms that continue operating quietly in the background even today.

A nation should have brave soldiers (physical courage) and wise statesmen (moral courage). One fights the battles, the other cultivates the relationships and policies that reduce their necessity. We need generals *and* conscientious objectors, because both are courageous warriors in their own way, fighting for important causes.

As we've said, half-cocked is not courage. "Macho" is often masochism. There's little bravery in spoiling for a fight and there's nothing impressive about playing Russian Roulette. There is zero glory in winning a battle—whether physical or verbal—to further immoral aims. And nothing is more immoral than unnecessary conflict.

Being right doesn't matter. It doesn't matter if you might lose face. Does anybody need to die over this? Does anybody need to lose their reputation over it? Could better decisions solve it in the future? What if somebody was willing to let the other person save face? What if *you* were that person?

These are heroic questions. If it can be avoided—it should be. Discretion, goes the expression, is the better part of valor.

It's part of valor because it takes courage—one has to be willing to look foolish, to be criticized, to take the hit, to do what they know is the right thing. Not everyone can do that. As the women's rights activist and suffragette Hannah Johnston Bailey explained, "A man has not the moral courage to plead for peace, for fear he shall be accused of effeminacy or cowardice." That was the trap of Lyndon Johnson in Vietnam. He knew it was a losing proposition, but he didn't want to look soft.

Hannah Johnston Bailey believed that women were uniquely suited for avoiding this. But why is that?

Perhaps it's empathy. Instead of thinking about how it will make them look, they are doing something more heroic, more selfless: They are thinking about what the consequences will be for other people.

If you operate from a place of fear or from selfishness, you'll miss this. You'll find yourself caught in an escalation trap. Nobody wins a war—metaphorical or literal. Sun Tzu would say that it is best to win without fighting—to have maneuvered in such a way that the enemy has lost before it has even begun.

That's right.

And by the way, that's how it worked out for Lincoln. Despite his valiant efforts, he could not stop those who preferred to "make war rather than let the nation survive." He did, through his restraint, however, manage to maneuver the South into its unwinnable role as the *aggressor* in the Civil War. The Southern leaders stupidly rushed themselves into firing the first shot in a war they claimed to be the victim of. It was a moral contradiction that they never overcame.

More important, they missed that they were hopelessly outmatched. They lacked the resources. They lacked the strategic vision. They lacked the allies and international support necessary to beat the North. They lacked an understanding of just how devastating and costly this rebellion would be. The South seized the initiative at the outset of the war, all the while Lincoln was coolly collecting these critical ingredients that would propel him to victory.

Yes, we must be willing to negotiate. We're willing to compromise. But run away? No. We avoid the petty fights so we can be ready for the ones that matter. When the South finally did bring war, Lincoln fought just as hard as Churchill and de Gaulle would generations later. He fought as hard as we must fight.

How do you square that circle? When to deescalate? When to charge in?

Whether it's a physical battle or a moral one, we follow

Shakespeare's advice in his famous "To thine own self be true" speech from *Hamlet:*

> Beware
> Of entrance to a quarrel, but being in,
> Bear 't that th' opposed may beware of thee.

You Must Go Through
the Wilderness

~

Seneca was exiled. Epictetus too. The twentieth-century German-American political philosopher Hannah Arendt was arrested by the Gestapo, spent eight days in prison, then seven years in exile. Galileo spent the remainder of his life under house arrest after daring to assert that the Earth revolves around the Sun and for refusing to retract this claim, even though no one would have blamed him if he had.

Eleanor Roosevelt was sent away by her parents as a young girl and then lived for decades in her husband's shadow. Herman Melville was savaged by reviewers. Steve Jobs was fired from Apple. Charles Darwin spent twenty-three years in purgatory before he could publish his thoughts about evolution.

You don't think that you'll be loved and appreciated for all you do, do you?

It'd be wonderful if we cherished our heroes, if we rolled out the red carpet for our creative geniuses. Instead, we put them through the gauntlet. We torture them. We drive them away.

Churchill was not only a prisoner of war in his youth, but at the height of his political career he was driven out of public life. His crime? In part, he was *right* about Germany. No one wanted another war. No one wanted him to be correct about Hitler's menace. So it was easier to make him go away than to prove him wrong.

For nearly ten years Churchill languished at his estate outside London. Or so his enemies thought. In fact, he was reading. He was writing. He was resting. He was making valuable contacts. He was waiting for his moment.

"Every prophet has to come from civilization," Churchill would explain, "but every prophet has to go into the wilderness. He must have a strong impression of a complex society . . . and he must serve periods of isolation and meditation. This is the process by which psychic dynamite is made."

Psychic dynamite is what Steve Jobs had. What Eleanor Roosevelt had. What Serpico and Florence Nightingale developed. They would not have had these things had their path been easier.

How long are you willing to be misunderstood? How long can you stand alone? Are you willing to be the only one in your company to go on the record? The only one in your party to voice the criticism? What are you willing to put up with to be true to what you believe? To do what you need to do?

For selfish reasons, Churchill could have quit, just as you can quit at any time. Churchill was fifty-four years old in 1929. He could have retired. Out of spite, he could have retreated to his own pursuits and pleasures.

He did not do that.

When England finally called, he wasn't just ready to answer, he had readied himself for precisely the crisis they called for him to solve. Churchill would be the explosive charge they—and the world—needed.

To go way out there on a limb? To fight for what you believe in? To be willing to suffer for your beliefs? These are both crucibles of courage . . . and breeding grounds for it. Few leaders are ever perfectly in sync with their times—they're usually ahead of them. Which is going to mean looking around and finding that they stand alone. Which is going to mean early moments of small crowds and few supporters.

What they can't do is moderate their beliefs for fear of being cast out of society. For the hope of fitting in.

No one wants to be driven away, but it may well be exactly what we need (which is in part why we can't let the *fear* of this outcome prevent us from doing what needs to be done day-to-day). Eventually, inevitably, if you are an independent, visionary, or principled person, you will find yourself alienated. Alienated from your peers. Alienated from the tenor of your times. You may be fired. You may be thrown out of office or made a pariah. Or, best-case scenario, humored but ignored.

You can let this break you, or you can let it form you—form you into the person that destiny is calling you to become. Because you know the work you're doing is important, because you know it's bigger than you.

De Gaulle would speak with special affinity for politicians who had to "cross the desert." He himself went through the desert not only in England during the war, but after it too. He spent twelve years out of power, from 1946 to 1958, while France convulsed and nearly destroyed itself. To restore her greatness again, de Gaulle was called to endure lonely years, powerless years, to be exiled in the desert. Even as France rejected him, he never gave up hope of saving her. This rejection, this failure, once again was how his psychic dynamite was made.

Remember: Between mountains lies the valley. You may have tumbled down from your former heights. You may have been thrown down. Or simply lost your way. But now you find yourself here. It is a low point. So?

A long desert. A desolate valley. Either way, you'll need to cross it. You'll need patience and endurance and most of all *love*. You can't let this period make you bitter. You have to make sure it makes you *better*.

Because people are counting on you.

Don't give up hope. Don't give up on *them*. They know not what they do. You, on the other hand, do know. This desert, this wilderness was given to you to cross. It's part of your journey.

To struggle makes the destination glorious. And heroic.

The Selflessness of Love

~

In the summer of 1969, Captain James Stockdale was forty-six years old. The brutal beatings and deprivations had been hard. He was struggling. He was scared.

All they wanted him to do was shave, to look presentable for the cameras. All they wanted him to do was go with them to sit in front of the cameras and say all was well.

Instead, James Stockdale used the razor they gave him to open a three-inch gash across his forehead. Sensing this wouldn't be enough, he grabbed a wooden stool and bashed his own face with it, repeatedly, until he could barely see.

Thus began his campaign of defiance against his captors in the Hanoi Hilton.

He wasn't a prisoner of war. He was a prisoner *at* war. And what he was fighting for was his men—even more than his country.

By the fall that year, as the torture of his comrades escalated,

Stockdale decided he was going to stop it. He would take one for the team. He would offer his life.

Tied to a chair, Stockdale waddled over to the only paned glass window in the prison and broke it. With a big shard of glass, he slit his wrists. "The last thing the North Vietnamese needed was me dead," he later wrote. "There had been a very solemn crowd of senior North Vietnamese officers in that room as I was revived. Prison torture, as we had known it in Hanoi, ended for everybody that night."

Twice, then, Stockdale had taken himself to the very brink. It was not for his benefit. He had no idea if he was going to survive the suicide attempt. He had a wife, children at home. He had his own hopes and dreams. He had so much to lose. Yet he was willing to trade that for the *hope* of alleviating somebody else's suffering?

The guards had not understood this. They thought they could pit the prisoners against one another. They thought they would all be in so much pain, so much fear, that they wouldn't much mind what was happening to somebody else. It's that old question, *But what about me?*

They were surprised to find, as Stockdale said, a sincere belief in an idea, an idea as old as the scriptures. "This idea is you are your brother's keeper," Stockdale said. "That's the flip side of 'What's in it for me?'"

To love thy neighbor is one thing. To be your brother's

keeper? To sacrifice for them? "Greater love hath no man than this," reads the Bible verse, "that a man lay down his life for his friends."*

Meanwhile, we're afraid to speak out for someone else's benefit because we *worked so hard* to get where we are.

A hero is not someone simply braving the elements, alone. It's not you against the world. It's not you *angry* at the world. It's about what you're willing to do *for* the world.

Think of Thích Quảng Đức in that same tragic conflict as Stockdale. Deeply distressed and angered by the South Vietnamese persecution of Buddhist citizens, he decided he would make an even more incredible gesture of defiance: *He lit himself on fire.* No one who has seen the photo can avoid being impacted by the insane courage of Thích Quảng Đức who sits in complete stillness and self-command, even as the flames consume his body.

It is almost too perfect that the root word of "courage" means "heart." Not only did Thích Quảng Đức's heart remain intact through his superhuman statement of resistance, but it survived the cremation process afterward as well. Today it sits displayed as a holy relic, a symbol of defiance.

What would make a person do something like that?

---

* The apostles *saw* Christ follow his own advice, painfully, by offering his life for all. Of the twelve apostles, it's thought that only one or two died a natural death.

It's not defiance for its own sake. Love. Love is the reason. A love of the innocent. A love of the future, even if they won't get to see it themselves.

Love makes us heroic.

Stockdale and his fellow POWs would signal back and forth to one another the letters U and S. What did it mean? *United States?* No: *Unity over Self.* They would say that to one another when they were lonely, when they were pulled away to be tortured, and when they sat in the cells beating themselves up for what they might have said under torture.

What unified whole are you a part of?

What is the love that's powering you?

Country? Cause? Comrade?

That's the flip side of *what about me.* That's how we rise above our limits.

Make People Bigger

~

There was Martin Luther King Jr. Most people have heard of him.

Fewer have heard about Ralph Abernathy, who gave up his parsonage at King's request to be his number two. Fewer still have heard of Stanley Levinson, who funded many of King's efforts, who wrote speeches for him, and when framed by the FBI as being some sort of communist spy, quietly and selflessly severed ties with King so no harm would come to the movement.

"I won't let Martin make that choice," he said when he'd heard that the president was threatening King over his association with Levinson. It was an incredibly painful blow, but he banished himself without question, without a whimper, refusing to even let his friend agonize over it.

In sports, there are two types of athletes. There are those generational talents, those feats of genetic and physical excellence who can make plays and take our breath away. Then there is another type, a little less gifted, a little less impressive to watch, but without them the game would not be possible.

These are the role players, the teammates, the leaders who bind the others together and give the team the *heart* they need to win. John Wooden talked about how it wasn't how tall you were but how tall you played. More impressive still is the athlete who makes the whole team taller. When we think of the Chicago Bulls, we think of Michael Jordan. We're forgetting Bill Cartwright, the captain who was literally and figuratively the center of the team for their first three consecutive championships.

Abernathy and Levinson made King taller. They made the movement stronger.

Can the same be said about you and the people around you?

Don't let your buddy down—that's the basis of military courage. But a hero goes beyond that. The essence of greatness is more than talent or skill. As Jackie Robinson said, a life is meaningless except for its impact on other lives. The athlete who makes their team better? An athlete who makes the team better *off* the court too? The leader who gets more out of the people around them? The artist who inspires their audience? The soldier whose calm is contagious?

That's what we're talking about.

Longfellow captured the true heroism of Florence Nightingale in a poem. It wasn't just her bravery, it wasn't just the deprivations she endured without complaint. It was what she did for people.

Honor to those whose words or deeds
Thus help us in our daily needs,
And by their overflow
Raise us from what is low.

She *made people bigger.* She made them better.

Standing at Thermopylae, the Hot Gates, in that stand of unity and selflessness, the Spartans made Greece bigger—spilling their blood to glue an alliance of the Greek states. Even de Gaulle's critics had to admit that's what the man had done: he willed France to stand tall at her lowest point.

We talked about how calm is contagious. Really, what we're doing is taking what we have a surplus of—in Nightingale's case it was compassion, in Abernathy's case it was courage, in Levinson's case it was business acumen—and we're spreading it around to the people who need it.

This can be done by example. We can provide inspiring words, as Churchill did. We can mentor, we can talk someone who wants to quit back from the ledge. We can deal in hope, reassure, lighten the load, firm up backbones. You can decide to do the unpleasant or difficult things others aren't willing to do because the team needs them done. You can be the one who says the truths that need to be said—to power, to the world, to a friend.

Remember: One drop starts the overflow. One play starts the comeback. One person saying one word can stop a retreat . . . or start one . . . can calm a mob or unleash one.

Anyone can be that person. You can give that work, make that play, be that drop.

Is it too on the nose to point out what word is contained inside en*courage*ment?

Longfellow talked about leaving footprints in the sands of time. But what's the point? The point is the trail this leaves.

Footprints, that perhaps another,
Sailing o'er life's solemn main,
A forlorn and shipwrecked brother,
Seeing, shall take heart again.

This is what heroes do. They make an impact. They make a difference for others. Today and forever.

Whether they're rewarded for this or not is not their concern. Success is not our motivation. "Happy is the man who can make others better," Seneca writes, "not merely when he is in their company, but even when he is in their thoughts." Even if this kills us, even if we're not around to enjoy the fruits of our sacrifice because it got us fired or killed or worse, it's still worth it. Our memory lives on in the mind of the witnesses.

That's who we were put here for anyway. Our duty was never just to *be* the best ourselves, but to help others realize their best. Even if, as is sometimes the case, this effort comes at our own expense.

No Time for Hesitating

~

As Mount Vesuvius erupted, those who could run away did. Those who were far away could see only the plumes of smoke and ash.

Pliny the Elder, an admiral and amateur scientist, was immediately curious. He planned to investigate until a messenger came with urgent news from a friend trapped at the foot of the mountain. Assembling the fleet, Pliny rushed to the scene in utter fearlessness to rescue all those he could by boat.

Arriving, he found the shoreline blocked by debris. A helmsman advised they turn back.

We talked before about how "fortune favors the bold." Do you know where that expression comes from? From Pliny, who refused to turn back. "'Fortes' 'fortuna iuvat: Pomponianum pete,'" he commanded. "Fortune favors the bold, head for Pomponianus," the friend he would save.

A few seconds of courage. No hesitation. Because he put his obligation to others above himself.

As his nephew recounted, what "he had begun in a spirit of

inquiry he completed as a hero." Tragically, Pliny did not survive. Fortune may *favor* the bold, but it offers no guarantee. The only certainty is that if we hesitate at the moment of crisis, we'll accomplish nothing and save no one.

Corporals Jonathan Yale and Jordan Haerter were working a guardpost in Ramadi in 2008 when a truck bomber raced toward the small base they protected. An exit to safety stood just a few feet away. The local police didn't hesitate to use it when they saw the truck coming. It was the two Marines, who had met only moments before, who stepped forward in unison and began to fire. Two thousand pounds of explosives went off as they unloaded their weapons into the accelerating truck.

Six seconds had elapsed between the time the truck entered the alley and its deadly blast.

The crater that marked the last moments of the two men's lives, just twenty and twenty-two years old, was more than sixty feet wide and five feet deep. General John Kelly, who interviewed witnesses on the scene, would write movingly of the sacrifice the heroes made without hesitation or consideration. "They could have run and likely survived, but did not," he said. "I do not think anyone would have called them cowards if they had. They took seriously the duties and responsibilities of a Marine on post, and stood their ground before they would allow anyone or anything to pass. For their dedication they lost their lives. Because they did what they did only two families had their hearts broken . . . rather than as many as fifty. These families will never know how truly close they came to a knock on the door that night."

Just a few seconds of courage—we talked about that. That's all it takes. It also may be all you have.

Yes, I'll donate the money, they need it—even though I can't afford it. *Yes, I'll assume the liability, somebody has to*—even though I could go to jail for it. *Yes, I'm going to quit my job so I can take care of my sick mother*—even though I have no idea how long it will take or what's waiting for me on the other side.

If you had more time, you'd overthink it. You'd come up with a reason. Your self-preservation would kick in. You'd be scared. You'd freeze.

And where does that leave your friends? Where does that leave your comrades? Your cause?

No, you have to go. You have to hit send. You have to push the child out of the way. You have to step forward. You have to speak up—there's not even time to clear your throat first.

You don't get to sleep on it. You don't get to run through all the scenarios. You don't get to ask for advice. Because people are counting on you. Because this is what you were trained for. Because this is what the situation demands, what your ideals demand.

Trust your gut. Do your duty.

Maybe it will work out. Maybe it won't.

The hero does it anyway.

As Kelly would say of those Marines—it was six seconds in

the alley. One second to recognize the situation. Two seconds to raise their weapons and fire. Two more critical seconds for the bullets to do their work and stop the truck. And just one fleeting second left to live, less than even what you've spent reading this sentence.

Six seconds.

"Not enough time to think about their families, their country, their flag, or about their lives or their deaths," Kelly later said, "but more than enough time for two very brave young men to do their duty . . . into eternity. That is the kind of people who are on watch all over the world tonight—for you."

Don't let them down.

We Make Our Own Luck

~

Sociologists and historians speak of something called "moral luck."

Not everyone finds themselves in a position to reveal some world-changing government secret. Not everyone is there when somebody falls into the water and can't swim. Not everyone who gets a call to go into nursing finds the field so primitive that even a little bit of knowledge can be revolutionary.

Not all of us are "lucky" enough to be of military age when Leonidas selected his three hundred, or to be a screenwriter called to testify against our colleagues in Hollywood, or to be a feminist during the suffragette movement. If that's what you want to call luck . . .

Churchill, writing of the statesman the Earl of Rosebery, noted with some sadness that the man lived in "an age of great men and small events." While there certainly was a kind of boring tranquility to the Victorian period (Rosebery lived from 1847 to 1929), it's also clear what a seductive rationalization this can be.

There were massive events in the middle of the nineteenth century, and great injustices cried out for help.

Where were these "great" men?

The United States didn't abolish slavery until 1865, Brazil until 1888. For the entirety of Rosebery's life, working conditions in England's factories were heinous and awful. Britain's colonial system and all its abuses carried on with few objections. The Irish question loomed over British politics and most leaders believed it hopeless. Countries regularly went to war for little reason and with little thought to the people affected. Millions starved. Millions were abused. Countless things went uninvented, unreformed, unchampioned.

There was plenty that *could have* been done in those years. It was true even within the great events of Churchill's time. Why didn't he tap himself on the shoulder about the Bengal Famine? Why did he so mishear Gandhi's moral call? Churchill had his finest hours but he can't escape the blame for those he was late to either. This remains true today. Whoever you are, wherever you live, whatever is going on. There's more you can do.

A hero is a person who does what needs to be done, not just for themselves but for others. That is, a hero makes their own luck—events don't just happen to them. Shakespeare said that we meet the time as it seeks us. But we have to seek the time and the moments too.

We can't be passive. We can't wait. We must reach out.

As Marcus Aurelius writes, "True good fortune is what you

make for yourself. Good fortune: good character, good intentions, and good actions."

Our hands are never as tied as we think. There is always something a hero can do, always someone they can help.

So, sure, we might not be put in de Gaulle's shoes, or Sophia Farrar's, or Frederick Douglass's. Our moment might not be as epic, and the stakes not as high. That's probably a good thing. But this does not exempt us.

We have to make our own luck, big or small. Just because we don't hear a voice like Nightingale, doesn't mean we aren't called to something, locally or globally.

Curse the darkness or light a candle? Bemoan the calm seas or build a motor?

We *will* our purpose into existence. We *choose* to be heroes.

And if we don't, it's on us.

Inspire Through Fearlessness

~

I t was, for a man famous for gambles, perhaps his biggest one.
On August 30, 1945, General Douglas MacArthur touched
down in Japan. A decade before his bold stroke in Korea, this
situation was just as dire. The fighting between the Allies and
the Axis powers had only just ceased. In six years of world war,
enemy boots had never trod on Japanese soil.

Every intelligence report warned of danger everywhere. Every
adviser suggested he wait.

And yet MacArthur proceeded into the heart of enemy territory, *unarmed.* As he watched his staff holstering pistols before
leaving headquarters for the flight to Tokyo, he had given the
order. "Take them off," he'd said. "If they intend to kill us, side-
arms will be useless. And nothing will impress them like a show
of absolute fearlessness. If they don't know they're licked, this
will convince them."

If one wonders how Japan so quickly made the unprece-
dented transition from suicidal warmonger to a peaceful, open
nation and unwavering ally of the country that broke its back,

this day is the answer. MacArthur landed and never betrayed a hint of fear or doubt. Every little gesture was deliberate—he ate without checking to see if his food was poisoned, he lifted martial law. He came in peace. He was completely confident.

It wasn't quite the same as facing artillery fire, but it likely required even more discipline and commitment. Churchill called it the single most courageous act of World War II. Never once did MacArthur think of his personal safety, only the groundwork for peace and reconstruction.

How many lives did this save? How many guerrillas did it deter? How much resistance did it prevent? Every island in the Pacific had been a bitter, deadly fight, but Tokyo itself went without a shot. MacArthur's entrance told them it was over . . . and they believed him. A more trepidatious commander could have never pulled it off, nor an angry or vengeful one.

Was there a moment—as they circled the runway, as he poked his head out of the plane for the first time, when he took the first bite of his dinner at a hotel staffed by people who would have killed him just days before—that MacArthur must have been terrified? That he might have wished he was back at headquarters? Of course, but for his men, for his country, for the cause of peace in the world, he had to put all that aside. He had to display complete and total fearlessness. He had to plunge ahead with poise.

All great leaders understand this. De Gaulle too practiced what he called *bain de foule*—plunging into the crowds of rapturous French citizens, bathing in their mutual spirit and love. Just as MacArthur's aides had warned against these public displays, de Gaulle's staff worried furiously about the safety of their leader, but he knew that it was precisely because it was so risky that it must be done.

The decision to walk down the Champs-Élysées after the liberation, even as snipers lurked and firefights still raged, helped free France. It gave purchase—at the potential cost of his life—to a relationship with the French people that he depended on for the rest of his career. It gave the French courage that sustains them still.

A leader cannot sit in some ivory tower or behind thick castle walls. They cannot protect themselves from every danger and risk while they let their followers or employees or soldiers take the brunt of what the world throws at us.

No, a leader must have real skin in the game. Whether that's putting their own money in the firm at a rock-bottom moment or riding in open-top cars, keeping the door to their office open, or sharing vulnerably what others would hide, the connection that is forged by such gestures provides far more safety than any risk avoidance can guarantee. The boss steps up to the microphones and answers every hostile question from the crowd—even the embarrassing ones about their own mistakes, taking the hit even for the stuff that wasn't their fault. The chief can't take up the rear, they lead the troops into battle. The parent doesn't just *tell* their kid to face their fears, they have to show them what it means to do that in their own life.

You must care about the people in your care. You must put them first. You must *show* them with your actions. Call them to something higher.

It was the moment when Martin Luther King Jr. went to jail that his followers saw he was more than just a preacher. He was *with* them. He risked his life *for* them. He was *one* of them.

We can't be afraid or we won't be able to do what needs to be done. But also, by this fearlessness—willingness to represent the cause, in the flesh, against all dangers—we show everyone else that they'll be okay as well.

The leader risks themselves *for* us. They step to the front. They make their courage contagious.

What Are You Willing to Pay?

~

"Better Red than dead" was Bertrand Russell's line. We're not supposed to judge another man's courage, but it's safe to say that this line, uttered not just from the protection of the ivory tower but quite possibly, in the case of the philandering Russell, from the bed of someone else's wife, is the pinnacle of cowardice.

For Russell, life was apparently more important than dignity. No principle, not even freedom, was worth more than self-preservation. He'd rather give way to Soviet totalitarianism than die.

Going back to Epicurus, some philosophers have questioned why one person would ever give their life for someone else's. They questioned risking for a cause, let alone dying for one. What's so bad about being a bootlicker, they ask, if it means you get to keep breathing? What good are principles if they cost you your life?

There's a logic to it. It's just a pathetic logic.

The (braver) philosopher John Stuart Mill would concede

that war was an ugly thing—ambition can be ugly too—but, he said, the "decayed and degraded state of moral and patriotic feeling which thinks that nothing is worth a war, is much worse." You have to care enough to draw the line somewhere, and the failure to do this is ultimately far uglier than most of the excesses of history.

The good news is that deep down we know there are things so much worse than dying. It's why we admire the heroes, famous or not, who fought and challenged, gambled and sacrificed for what they believed in.

Cato gave his life to resist Julius Caesar. Thrasea and, belatedly, Seneca fell in opposition to Nero. The Spartans preferred to fight as free men than live as rich slaves under Xerxes. Isn't that what we recognize in Socrates's greatness? He could have gotten away, bribed his way out of jail, but he didn't. And Jesus too?

Let us pause for a moment to memorialize some lesser-known heroes: The nameless blacks who were beaten, who lost jobs, had their loans called in but still registered to vote anyway. The countless couples who married interracially in defiance of the Nazis or apartheid. A sixty-year-old mother named Lori Gilbert-Kaye who threw herself in front of her rabbi during a mass shooting in 2019, shielding him from death with her body and her life. Leonard Roy Harmon, a black cook on a Navy ship who used his body to protect the evacuated wounded at Guadalcanal, dying for a country that was still illegally depriving him of his ability to vote and live freely. Anne Dufourmantelle, the French philosopher, who died rescuing two drowning children while on vacation. Wilfred Owen, the poet quoted earlier in this book, who returned to active service in World War I after his friend and fellow poet Siegfried Sassoon had been seriously wounded. Like Bertrand Russell, Owen was antiwar, but he felt *someone* should document the horrors of the war. He would die in battle just a week before the Armistice, dying in a war he opposed, but fulfilling a duty he believed he had.

"We should cherish the body with the greatest care," Seneca said. Same goes for our profession, our standing, the life we have built for ourselves. "We should also be prepared, when reason, self-respect, and duty demand the sacrifice, to deliver it even to the flames."

We said before that fear asks, "But what if . . .?" It worries about the cost—mostly to ourselves. A hero doesn't think about that. They accept the bill that comes due for doing the right thing.

Think of an aging leader who retires to make room for the next generation (as General Mattis tried to do in 2016 or Lou Gehrig did the second he felt his play decline). Think of a politician who cuts their own political throat to pass necessary legislation (Lyndon Johnson signing the Civil Rights Act: "I think we just gave the South to the Republicans," he said). Think of the artist who offends the audience or the patron to pursue their creative calling (at the peak of his career, Norman Rockwell walked away from his obscenely lucrative *Saturday Evening Post* cover gig in pursuit of more artistic freedom . . . which he promptly used to paint his most haunting and moving pieces about racism in America). It's estimated that protesting the draft cost Muhammad Ali more than $10 million in career earnings.

During the COVID-19 pandemic, some businesses were willing to sacrifice for public health, while some were not. It seems like an obvious trade, but if it were so obvious, everyone would have done it.

We talked about the courage of business leaders who make hard choices, but perhaps the hardest choice for a company is to make a decision that prioritizes people over profits. It took courage for Reed Hastings to jettison his DVD business, but it'd have been braver had he stood up to Saudi Arabia when they demanded the removal of a controversial Netflix show that criticized their government for murdering a dissident journalist. Instead, thinking of his stock price, Hastings explained, "We're not trying to do 'truth to power.' We're trying to entertain."

What good is being a billionaire if you can't use it to take the pretty straightforward stance against *dismembering members of the press*?

All businesses, like people, have competing duties. But ultimately there are things bigger than dollars, and as humans we answer to something beyond the boardroom, like when CVS stopped selling cigarettes, even though tobacco products earned the chain some $2 billion per year. It's not quite Jonas Salk declining to patent the polio vaccine, but it is impressive. As it happens, it actually did make a difference. Because customers didn't simply shop elsewhere, many of them just quit smoking. Tobacco sales fell industry-wide—even though no other major retailers followed suit—all because one store was willing to sacrifice revenue for what was right.

Taking the hit for someone, something else. That's what heroes do. A coward thinks of themselves.

Courage forces us to ask, "If not now, when?" and "If not me, then who?" It pushes us to be bold. It also asks: What if everyone was selfish? What would things look like? It encourages us to gamble on ourselves, to carve out an unconventional path. But we can't forget the other side of the rabbi Hillel's question is equally important. "If I am only for me," he asks, *"who am I?"*

We resist the creeping pull of nihilism, we assert our agency over chance and fate, but why? It cannot be merely for our own survival. The poet Maya Angelou once said that courage is about standing up for yourself *and* for others.

That's what we're doing here. In fact, *that is why we are here.*

The Big Why

To push past her parents' objections, past the judgments of society, to spend time in the wilderness, to follow the call? We understand that this took immense courage from Florence Nightingale, just as it would for any boy or girl in a small town to chase their dreams in the big city.

Imagine the agents and advertisers trying to convince Michael Jordan not to walk away from basketball for baseball. When Jeff Bezos explained to his Wall Street boss the idea for Amazon, his boss took him for a walk and said, "It's a good idea but it would be a better idea for somebody who doesn't already have a job."

Would we admire Florence as much if the purpose of her break had been solely to settle into a life as a nineteenth-century bohemian? If Pat Tillman had quit football to become a venture capitalist? It takes courage to depart from the conventional path; it's heroic when you do it for selfless reasons.

Maya Moore made it to the top of her field. She won four WNBA rings. She was a six-time All-Star. She has a scoring title, a steals title, as well as a Rookie of the Year award and a Wooden Award.

But then she hit pause and walked away. Not to make more money in television, not to enjoy a break from the grind—no, it was to free a man unjustly behind bars. And she succeeded. Now they're married.

David Brooks has talked about the "second mountain"—the thing we dedicate ourselves to climbing for reasons beyond just the courageous love of a good challenge or the rewards that go along with defying the odds that deterred everyone else. The mountain we climb after braving the difficulties of the first mountain and realizing that just being successful is not all that fulfilling.

When we separate courage from heroism, it's partly around this distinction. It's not just that the cause makes all, it's that there is something altogether different about dedicating yourself to something that may well be *in conflict* with your self-interest.

The greater the sacrifice, the greater the glory. Even if the achievements don't seem so notable . . .

. . . the mother who puts her dream aside to care for her sick child.

. . . the immigrant who puts on an apron each day despite their foreign medical degree.

. . . the employee who quits a high-paying or high-status job in an industry they now believe is making the world a worse place.

... the person whose reputation unfairly takes a public beating as they silently protect someone else.

Moore's decision meant walking away from millions of dollars, from being on television, from the prime years of her career. What was *right* had the potential to cost her everything ... and she did it anyway.

People doubted her. They criticized her. Surely, the consensus was not that the man she wanted to free was innocent—if it was, the legal battle wouldn't have taken all those years. She braved this. The upside was not certain. The downside was the future of her career and life.

"Character," de Gaulle reflected at the end of his life, "is above all the ability to disregard insults or abandonment by one's own people. One must be willing to lose everything. There is no such thing as half a risk."

That's a damn good definition of heroism too.

To Go Back to the Valley

~

In 1939, Dietrich Bonhoeffer made it safely to America. From his pulpit, he had watched Hitler's rise with horror, and now he was safe. Yet almost immediately after entering New York harbor, he began to have regrets. Every thought was of Germany, of the people he'd left behind, of what use he might have been able to be.

It was like being on vacation while his country burned.

Finally, he decided: He would return. "I have come to the conclusion that I made a mistake in coming to America," he explained. "I must live through this difficult period in our national history with the people of Germany. I will have no right to participate in the reconstruction of Christian life in Germany after the war if I do not share the trials of this time with my people . . . Christians in Germany will have to face the terrible alternative of either willing the defeat of their nation in order that Christian civilization may survive or willing the victory of their nation and thereby destroying civilization. I know which of these alternatives I must choose but I cannot make that choice from security."

As Hitler plunged Europe into war, Bonhoeffer chose voluntarily to plunge himself into his own war against Hitler, even though he must have sensed, even known, that to go back was to willingly go to the gallows.

He would eventually be arrested, imprisoned, and hanged for conspiring against Hitler—having quite nearly succeeded at assassinating history's greatest monster. The inscription on the monument that honors Bonhoeffer and his coconspirators reads simply: "In resistance against dictatorship and terror, they gave their lives for freedom, justice and humanity."

Incredible courage is required of the immigrant and the refugee. To leave one's home behind, to try to provide your family a better life? But just as it is some people's destiny to cross oceans and deserts, it may be our destiny to *stay*, literally or figuratively.

Frank Serpico's mother sought greener pastures on the other side of the rough Atlantic waters. Serpico, caught in the corruption of the NYPD and the toxic culture that allowed it, must have fantasized countless times about quitting. He stayed and he fought . . . even after they shot him in the face for testifying.

Why should I quit? he said. *I'm not the one doing anything wrong.*

Alexey Navalny stayed in Russia despite grave political and personal risk. Xu Zhiyong might have found a way to leave China, but he didn't. It's always a bit baffling to outsiders when these dissidents are eventually arrested, or, in Navalny's case, nearly assassinated, and then—returning again after he recovered, saying goodbye to his wife as she wiped away his tears—facing a travesty of justice as he continued to fight for the soul of his country.

Why didn't they get out?

The answer, as it often is with reformers, is that they believed they could do more good by staying than going, by returning than living in exile. They were willing to run the risks. They knew how the powers that be would respond, and they were brave enough to take their stands anyway. The singer and social activist Paul Robeson was asked why he didn't flee a racist America for a more welcoming Europe. "Because my father was a slave," he said, "and my people died to build this country, and I am going to stay right here and have a part of it [. . .] And no Fascist-minded people will drive me from it. Is that clear?"

This is why we show up for work every day even though we aren't wanted. Even though it's dangerous. We aren't the one in the wrong, so why should we be driven away? If other people want to leave, want to quit, if other people have decided there is no future, just know you don't have to agree. You can stay. You can go back.

In fact, that might be the most courageous thing you can do.

When we sacrifice like this, as Robeson did, as Navalny did, we call others to follow our lead, whether that's refusing to abandon a friend whose personal crisis has made them radioactive or sticking with a line of inquiry we know will bear fruit, even if everyone has lost faith. Let everyone else flee—we're not going to be deterred that easily. We're not going to abandon our political party or our hometown, we're going to stay and fix it. Because we know it's the right thing to do.

As the police cracked down during the bus boycott, Martin Luther King Jr. got away to Atlanta. He was free. He was safe. His father and others pleaded for him to remain there, leading the cause from afar. "I must go back to Montgomery," King told them. "I would be a coward to stay away. I could not live with myself if I stayed here hiding while my brothers and sisters were being arrested in Montgomery." This was the commitment of his life. Once he became a marked man, he could have stayed in the North and led the civil rights movement and lived to be an old man. Instead, as he would say repeatedly in his speeches, he would "go back to the valley." His mission obligated him . . . and his faith guided him.

Sometimes we are called to go. But sometimes destiny demands that we stay—that we go back willingly into the jaws, that we stay and fight. For our jobs, our cause, or our life. For our family. For our neighbors.

And heroes do this at great cost to themselves.

Silence Is Violence

~

One of the conspirators against Nero was caught and interrogated: *Why did you do this?*

"Because," the soldier replied to the emperor who had been consumed by his demons and delusions, "it was the only way I could help you."

You hear the same thing said to whistleblowers and truthtellers and activists of all kinds. *Why are you being like this? Don't you see the trouble this is causing? Do you have to make such a big deal out of this? Why won't you let us wash our own laundry?*

The answer is: Because they love too much. They care too much. They care about "it" more than they care about themselves. And to say nothing or do nothing is to actually do more harm than whatever discomfort comes by being such a stickler, or by drawing public attention to an unpleasant issue.

At a critical moment in the Korean War, a young assistant spoke up to Secretary of State Dean Acheson. He worried that the orders for MacArthur, drawn up by the Joint Chiefs of Staff, were too vague—that their uncertainty would create an opportunity for MacArthur to needlessly escalate the war. "For God's sake," a very busy and flustered Acheson replied, "how old are you? Are you willing to take on the Joint Chiefs?"

The assistant, just thirty-two, was not. So he took his objections no further. His career was more important.

Just days later, the Chinese, triggered by MacArthur's aggressive moves, flooded troops into Korea. World War III almost began.

When we decline to get involved, to risk ourselves or our reputations, we have to understand that it is not just our own careers or life at stake. Two thousand years ago, long before the famous quote about what evil needs to prevail, Marcus Aurelius was reminding himself that "you can also commit injustice by doing nothing."

Do you want to think about a world where Florence Nightingale did *not* revolutionize nursing? Because she didn't want to piss off her parents, because she didn't want to confront the bureaucrats in charge? Where de Gaulle stayed on Pétain's staff, where the Spartans did not take their stand at Thermopylae because they got a sweet deal for themselves?

We might not be here had they decided to think of themselves first, if they had kept quiet.

We certainly would not be here were it not for the cumulative sacrifices of the artists who pushed past the censors, the scientists who challenged the church, the inventors who went public with warnings, the protestors who proceeded despite the mobs and the dogs.

It's worth noting: Not all of these men and women survived their courageous journeys.

The unfortunate reality is that sometimes the right thing is a kamikaze mission, usually not literally, most often figuratively so. Sometimes our lance must be broken against the shield. Sometimes we must be willing to go all the way. We must be willing to lose the job, lose the client, lose our good standing, break from our friends, make the sacrifice.

Of course, that's scary. We are up against our fear and our instinct for self-preservation.

But we have been cultivating courage in our lives for a reason. It wasn't just so we could be a little more successful. It wasn't just so we could experience the things life had to offer, the things on the other side of fear.

We cultivate courage so we can do important work that people are counting on.

As Martin Luther King Jr. said, "A time comes when silence is betrayal."

He knew this personally. For he owed Kennedy for the call that saved him from time on a chain gang or a lynching, but also Sargent Shriver, Kennedy's brother-in-law, who had spoken up for it. Several of Kennedy's campaign men had warned him not to intervene. Kennedy had been deterred by their warnings. Shriver decided it was worth risking everything to get through. "I never use my family connections or ask for a favor, but you are wrong, Kenny," he told Kennedy's top campaign adviser. "This is too important. I want time alone with him."

There, in a hotel room, his access and his reputation on the line, Shriver managed to appeal to Kennedy's moral compass. He persevered until he got through, even though he had been warned, "If it works, you'll get no credit for it; if it does not, you'll get all the blame." In fact, that was his reward: He was yelled at first for costing Kennedy the campaign . . . and after the election results proved him right, his role was immediately forgotten. All downside, no upside . . . and yet he braved it.

It's heroic to take that bad bargain.

If we don't do the right thing, who will? And if somebody doesn't do it, how many will suffer?

We can't keep silent. We can't remain passive.

We have to be willing to take them on.

It's the only way we can help.

The Audacity of Hope

～

In 1961, John Lewis was knocked unconscious by a man for trying to use a "Whites Only" waiting room at a bus stop in South Carolina. It was one of many senseless beatings that Lewis received in his courageous campaigns as a Freedom Rider and civil rights activist. This one, like any of the others, could have easily been the one that finally broke his heart and spirit. Here he was, expecting only the most minimal human decency, and people were trying to kill him over it. In fact, quite a few friends and far too many innocent children would and had been brutally murdered for daring to insist on their constitutional rights.

How could that not affect a person? How could it not close them off? Yet forty-eight years later, Lewis had the chance to meet his attacker, a man named Elwin Wilson, face-to-face. Because Wilson was ready to apologize.

More surprisingly, Lewis was willing to accept it.

Most of us would give up on humanity after the first or fourth or fifteenth beating. How many times could we endure going to jail? (John Lewis was arrested forty-five times!) How many years of stalled progress could we endure? Wouldn't it be natural to feel anger and despair?

Love? Compassion? Optimism? Ever letting our guard down again? Get out of here.

Just about the craziest, bravest thing you can do in this damned world of ours is to keep hoping.

Because there are so many reasons not to:

The pain.

The failures.

The good guys who get punished.

The unrelenting parade of greed and selfishness, stupidity, and hate.*

It's so easy to say, "What's the point?"

But if we give up, we lose.

You can't win a battle or make a change you've quit on.

John Lewis refused to quit. With Elwin Wilson in his office, he inscribed a book to his former abuser. "To Elwin Wilson: With faith and hope. Keep your eyes on the prize."

There was something to that faith. When you believe in something, it makes it easier to believe in people. It's what helps you endure the pain and the shortcomings. Besides, could anyone

---

*It's funny that the nihilists, with their expectations already at nothing, always seem to be so damn disappointed in people.

have scripted a more perfect detail than the fact that *Hope* was in fact Wilson's middle name?

"Work, love, courage and hope," a young Anne Frank wrote to herself. "Make me good and help me cope!" If she didn't quit on humanity, even then, in an *attic* hiding from storm troopers, what excuse do we have?

Not specific hope: *Oh, this will be over by December. Oh, we're about to turn the corner. Oh, all my pain will magically go away.* Not silly fantasies either ("If you can dream—and not make dreams your master."). Hope has to be deeper, more profound. It's the hope of Shackleton, that he would survive against the odds and come back to rescue his men. Of de Gaulle, that although he was alone, eventually, if he kept at it, eventually that would cease to be so. It's this hope that can become an effective truth.

Even after the divorce, even after the robbery, even after the unexpected failure and the subsequent bankruptcy, we can't quit—not on people, not on the belief in a better future. *I refuse to accept that the vault of justice is bankrupt. I refuse to accept that man is unredeemable. I refuse to accept that I can't make this better. I will not stop until I create some meaning out of this suffering.*

Not believing in hope is a cop-out. It's nihilism, as we've talked about, a dark reason not to have to care or try. But to hope? To hope is an obligation. It's also a light. Hope is the thing with feathers, as Emily Dickinson said. It perches on our soul. It guides us through the storm. It keeps us warm. She also says it doesn't ask anything of us.

But that's not quite right. Hope asks for courage *and then some*.

We carry the fire, at risk of being burned. We are of good cheer, despite the horror and the despair. We keep our hearts open, after we've had it broken. We proceed, ignoring the horrendous odds.

Hope powers us, and by spreading this hope we perform a heroic act.

Remember: Leaders are dealers in hope. Nobody wants to live in a world without a tomorrow, without a reason to continue, without some dot on the horizon they're aiming at. And if we want that, we're going to have to *make* it. For them and for ourselves, heroically.

Whatever we do, we cannot surrender to bitterness. We must reject the heresy of despair. We can't give up on ourselves or on other people. We have to tell ourselves a story—about history, about our lives—that emphasizes agency, progress, the chance of redemption.

We hope against hope against hope. That is the seed of all greatness.

It is the key to a better tomorrow.

You Must Burn the White Flag

Endurance is one thing. Refusing to surrender is another.

There is a story about Epictetus, under torture by his master, who expected him to beg him to stop, calmly warning him over and over again that his leg was about to break. Finally, it snapped. "What did I tell you?" he said.

It was this commitment, this perseverance that transcends simple endurance. Epictetus could not, would not allow his spirit to be broken, he would not give in to bitterness or hopelessness. And that's how he eventually survived thirty years of slavery and an exile to boot.

Cato not only refused to surrender to Caesar as he fought to preserve the Roman Republic, he demanded that no one ask for mercy or clemency on his behalf. Because that would mean he had been beaten, that he had been conquered by the forces of tyranny, and that was not the case.

That's what a hero does. They burn not only the boats behind them, but the white flag too.

Emmeline Pankhurst in her famous "Freedom or Death"

speech—inspired by Cato and his own resistance—outlined this kind of commitment.

> As long as women consent to be unjustly governed, they can be, but directly women say: We withhold our consent, we will not be governed any longer so long as that government is unjust. Not by the forces of civil war can you govern the very weakest woman. You can kill that woman, but she escapes you then; you cannot govern her. No power on earth can govern a human being, however feeble, who withholds his or her consent.

We understand that while there may be some situations that call for a tactical retreat, we never, ever *surrender*.

They can count you out.

They can throw you in chains.

They can confiscate your property.

They can humiliate you in the press.

They can attack you in court.

They can throw the full might of their corporate resources at you.

They can banish you to a rock in the middle of the ocean.

They can take a lot away from you, but as long as you're alive, they can't *make* you quit.

Rioters burned the bus the Freedom Riders came in on. Do

you know what the riders did? *They boarded the next bus.* They got stitched up in the hospital and kept going. Because they had something they were fighting for.

"If you see the president," Grant told a reporter as he bore down on Lee, "tell him for me that, whatever happens, there will be no turning back." He wasn't sure he could win, but he was saying, like the Spartans, that he was going to come back with his shield or on it. No one can truthfully promise victory, so what Grant was pledging was to give everything it was possible for him to give—including his life.

"Stoics belittle physical harm, but this is not braggadocio," James Stockdale wrote. "They are speaking of it in comparison to the devastating agony of shame they fancied good men generating when they knew in their hearts that they had failed to do their duty vis-à-vis their fellow men or God."

It's from the soul that the hero draws their real power. It's not about who has a bigger army, the better weapons, or who has the stronger case or the bigger budget. The one who won't ever quit will be the winner, if not now, then later, if not in this life, then in the next.

Si succiderit, de genu pugnat. If his legs fail, still he fights on his knees. Still they rise, even if it's not literally possible.

Churchill wasn't *sure* that Britain could hold out. Nobody could have been. He was sure about how *he* would respond if the Nazis came. *What should we do?* his daughter-in-law asked.

Nothing is stopping you from getting a carving knife from the kitchen, he told her, *nothing can stop you from taking a few of the bastards out with you.*

No one is saying they can't eventually beat you, only that surrender is a choice. Quitting on your cause—that's on you.

Resistance unto . . . whatever you've got left to give.

Hemingway reminds us that while it is certainly possible to be destroyed—by life, by the enemy, by a bad break—no one can *defeat* us. That's our call. That's in our power. And it only happens when we give up. The only way to lose is to abandon your courage.

Defeat is a choice. The brave never choose it.

No One Is Unbreakable

~

We think that courage means being unbreakable.
   Nah.

It means getting back up when you've been broken.

Because your kids are watching.

Because the cause needs you.

Because you won't let evil triumph.

It means putting yourself back together so you can do what needs to be done, for yourself, for others.

But some of us are afraid to do that. Not afraid to keep going, but afraid to be vulnerable enough to admit we're wounded, that we need repair, that we've been dealt a setback.

In one of Hemingway's most beautiful passages, he writes:

If people bring so much courage to this world the world has to kill them to break them, so of course it kills them. The world breaks every one and afterward many are strong at the broken places. But those that will not break, it kills. It kills the very good and the very gentle and the very brave impartially.

The world is a cruel and harsh place. One that, for at least four and a half billion years, is undefeated. From entire species of apex predators to Hercules to Hemingway himself, it has been home to incredibly strong and powerful creatures. And where are they now? Gone. Dust. Too many of them before their time, unnecessarily so.

Because they confused strength with resilience.

Stoicism—deep, deep courage—is there to help you recover when the world breaks you and, in the recovering, to make you stronger at a much more profound level. The Stoic heals themselves by focusing on what they can control: Their response. The repairing. The learning of the lessons. Preparing for the future. Making a difference for others. Requesting help. Changing. Sacrificing for a greater good.

This is not an idea exclusive to the West. There is a form of Japanese art called *kintsugi,* which dates back to the fifteenth century. In it, masters repair broken plates and cups and bowls, but instead of simply fixing them back to their original state, they make them better. The broken pieces are not simply glued together, but instead fused with a special lacquer mixed with gold or silver. The legend is that the art form was created after a broken tea bowl was sent to China for repairs. But the returned bowl was ugly—the same bowl as before, but cracked. *Kintsugi* was invented as a way to turn the scars of a break into something beautiful.

That's the question the world is asking sometimes. It knows we're brave, so it wants to know: Death or *kintsugi*?

Will you find a way to become stronger at the broken places? Or will you so cling to your old ways that you will be shattered?

A hero gets back up. They heal. They grow. For themselves and others.

Audie Murphy concludes his memoir with this idea. He has been damaged by war. He knew it. He has seen things he shouldn't have to see. Like many veterans and trauma survivors, he has PTSD. But he decides that this will not define him. "Suddenly, life faces us," he writes. "I swear to myself that I will measure up to it. I may be branded by war, but I will not be defeated by it."

I will go home, he says. He is not going to give up. He will not let his demons win. He will find his dream girl, get married, start a family. He will find a new career, a new purpose. "I will learn to look at life through uncynical eyes," he says to himself, just as you must, "to have faith, to know love. I will learn to work in peace as in war. And finally—finally, like countless others, I will learn to live again."

Courage Is Virtue.
Virtue Is Courage.

~

The virtues are like music. They vibrate at a higher, nobler pitch.

I n the beginning," Goethe opens his play *Faust*, "there was the Word."

Then he corrects himself. No, in the beginning there was the *deed*.

This has been a book about courage, the first in a series about the cardinal virtues. Here at the end of it, it's worth pointing out: Words don't matter. *Deeds do*.

Nothing proves this more, in fact, than the relationship between courage and the other three virtues of temperance, justice, and wisdom. These things are impossible, worthless even, without courage to secure them.

As C. S. Lewis wrote, "Courage is not simply *one* of the virtues, but the form of every virtue at the testing point." Try living with moderation. Try being honest. Try pursuing knowledge. Try doing any of these things in a world that has forsaken wisdom and self-discipline and justice and you'll see.

See how far you get without courage. You will be mocked. You will be criticized. You will be undermined. You will be impeded. You will find your bank balance approaching zero. All of this is a test.

Without courage, you won't pass. The mob will get you . . . or you will become part of the mob. The strain will break you . . . or you will break your commitments to what is causing the strain.

Courage is the only way. It's the backbone of all the rest.

You're gonna need it.

Because, look, talking about virtue is easy. It flowed well onto these pages, buttressed by centuries of poetry and literature and memories. But the purpose of writing this book, and the hours you spent reading it, was not mere entertainment.

We are trying to actually get better. We are trying to answer our own call, make that Herculean choice ourselves. Today. Tomorrow. At every moment.

What good will any virtue be if it exists only on paper? What's the point if you don't have the courage to live it? To stand alone with it? To insist on it even with so many rewards to the contrary?

Sure, there is a relationship between study and practice, but at some point the rubber meets the road. We contemplate truth and then we have to act on it. We absorb in into our souls. The ancients were fond of an expression: *Character is fate.*

It meant that what you believed determined what you would do. The four virtues were about instilling character—good character—so that at the critical point, a person could act on instinct. Courage is not something you declare, like bankruptcy, it is something you earn, that becomes part of you. Just as a writer becomes one by writing—and a great writer by writing that which is worth reading—"courageous" is a superlative paid for over the course of a life of courageous decisions.

The people we have followed so far—from Charles de Gaulle to Leonidas, Frederick Douglass, Theodore Roosevelt, Eleanor Roosevelt, Marcus Aurelius, Sophia Farrar, Frank Serpico, James Stockdale—they were not perfect. At times they exhibited the exact opposite of the virtues we are studying, and that must be noted. Still, it cannot be denied that at a key, critical moment, their *character* propelled them to do something profoundly great. Not just then, for the people they helped or the cause they furthered, but also for us, today, in the inspiration that this provides.

It wasn't their words that mattered. It was who they were.

That's what Lincoln expressed at Gettysburg: It doesn't matter what we say here, it matters what *they did there.* Whether it was at Thermopylae in 480 BC, or with British troops two thousand years later in the same pass with the same table stakes against the Germans, whether it was Florence Nightingale answering her call or Maya Moore answering hers, whether they understood fully the sacrifice they were making or the consequences of the stand they were taking, their courage echoes on down.

Their virtue shines.

We cannot consecrate it. It stands eternal on its own. A sacrifice delivered even to the flames.

Because we know we wouldn't be here were it not for the bravery of those who came before it.

There is only one way we can repay them for this.

It's by adding to it our own deeds, by picking up their "unfinished work." We must continue the tradition we have been part of, whether we know it or not. We must follow Hercules.

It begins by choosing virtue. Not virtue signaling, but virtuous *living*.

We can learn about virtue all we want, but when we get to the crossroads, there we will have to make a choice.

We opened this book with the Bible and with John Steinbeck. Let us close by bringing them together. In Steinbeck's *East of Eden,* he concludes that the most powerful phrase in Christianity is *timshel*. When we read the commandments translated into English, they are rendered as just that, *commandments*. But Steinbeck thinks the Hebrew rendering is more accurate, not "Thou shalt" but "Thou mayest."

"Here is individual responsibility and the invention of con-science," he reflected to his editor as he wrote those pages. "You can if you will but it is up to you. This little story turns out to be one of the most profound in the world. I always felt it was, but now I know it is."

Whether it's from the Bible or from Hercules or *East of Eden* or *Faust,* the parable's message is the same: *We have a choice.* We *choose* between cowardice and courage, virtue and vice.

Courage calls us in our fear. It calls us to each act of bravery and perseverance our duties require. And it calls us beyond our-selves to a greater common good.

It's our decision how to answer the call. Not just once but a thousand times in a life. Not just in the past and the future but right now, today.

What will it be?

Can you be brave? Who and what will you be brave for?

The world wants to know.

Afterword

~

I was maybe twenty-three years old when Dov Charney, the CEO of American Apparel, asked me to leak naked photos of a woman who was suing him.

I told him I would not.

He believed these pictures and the accompanying text messages would exonerate him. To a certain extent he was right. They also constituted what we now call "revenge porn."

I said I wanted no part in it.

At the time, I felt a certain satisfaction with myself for this moment of moral courage. As I've gotten older, and having written the pages you've just read, the choice holds up but also seems shamefully insufficient. On the one hand, defying Dov Charney was not something people did at American Apparel: not if they wanted to keep their job, let alone stay on the boss's good side. On the other hand, why didn't I turn around, walk out the door, and never look back? Why didn't I quit on the spot? Why didn't everybody? Why did I *still* want to keep the job?

I remember walking into his office a few weeks later and

witnessing a video call between him and reporters from major media outlets where they viewed the photos. I had stopped only my participation in the scheme. I had done nothing to actually prevent it from happening. Within minutes, they would be splashed across the internet and the press.

Why did my courage fail me?

It's a question I have asked myself many times since. Because that was not the only moral quandary I found myself in at American Apparel. I told myself that I stayed over the years because I wanted to protect the people who worked for me. I stayed because I thought I could make more of a difference by staying. Because I believed in the mission of the company (it was doing good in the world). Because I wasn't like the others or *like him*. To a certain extent that was true. But we can always find reasons not to do the hard but right thing. At that age, walking away from money, from the most important job I'd ever had, disrupting the plans I had for my life—those all weighed very heavily on me.

The irony, in retrospect, was that at the very moment I was already making plans to do something much scarier: to transition away from the corporate world and become a writer. I believe I was afraid of what severing my lifeline would mean. I hesitated over being without a salary. I was deterred by the uncertainty, by the leap in the dark. But in hesitating, I put myself and my safety above what was right, and above other people.

For three more years, I remained with the company as an adviser and a strategist, which mostly consisted of running interference for the employees whom I could help and preventing the car from crashing into a ditch. I prevented bad decisions from being made. I steered decisions in a more ethical direction. I tried to rein Dov in. I kept the thing going in my small way, helping thousands of garment workers to keep making a living wage. I also continued to get paid, and as a result, I can't fully escape complicity for the bad that did happen.

A profile in courage I was not.

In 2014, after I had established myself as a writer of three books, events took a sudden turn. Dov, whose grasp on reality had been intermittent before, spiraled. He was living on a cot in the warehouse. He struck an employee. He would rant like a lunatic. He had driven the stock price to the lowest it had ever been. The lawsuits continued because he could not stop himself.

During Dov's descent into madness, I frequently had discussions with some of American Apparel's board members about the state of affairs inside the company. As the reports grew worse, the board eventually decided to move on their CEO. I began to argue that Dov needed help in the way that Nero had needed help—that *removing* him was the only way to do it. It had taken me too long to get there, but once I made the decision, there wasn't any doubt it was the right path. On the day I ended my book tour for *The Obstacle Is the Way,* I got a call from Dov and then from his number two. The board had finally fired him.

Could I have made a difference if I had advocated for this earlier? Or would I have been fired? If I had quit in protest in

2011, would it have sent a message or gone without notice? If I hadn't held my fire, I wouldn't have been around for the pivotal moment when it did come. Or . . . that's what I tell myself.

Dov, unaware of my efforts, tried to purchase my loyalty in those desperate moments. *I will buy you a publishing imprint,* he told me. Could he have delivered on that promise? Probably not. It didn't matter because I was not interested. I had crossed my Rubicon. I flew to Los Angeles and began a new role trying to rebuild the company and save it from Dov, who instead of walking away with millions decided that if he couldn't be in charge he'd rather attack what he'd spent his life building. It was a race to stop him from burning the whole place down.

There was a hostile takeover from Wall Street and then a poison pill from the board. It was hardly time in a war zone, but it was chaos at a level I had never seen. I had to brave criticism and intrigue and all sorts of other nonsense. I would sit and be interviewed for a number of investigations. I showed them where bodies had been buried and money had been wasted. I convinced other people to share their stories and protected them from retaliation. I cleaned up long-standing messes and canceled policies that never should have been put in place. I comforted people. I tried to make things right. I worked long hours, far from home, while my wife waited patiently alone, as we attempted to salvage the ruins of the company. It was exhausting.

But not every battle is able to be won. The new corporate leadership hesitated at a critical moment. There were employees who needed to be fired—who had been corrupted over the years. When they were kept on, out of fear of upsetting anyone, Dov was able to sabotage the company through them. Then the hedge fund that bought the company relented under his pressure and brought Dov partly back into the fold. I had warned against this repeatedly, so I quit on the spot, giving up the rest of my contract.

He had been fired for reasons that had been denied and excused for too long. The idea of then reversing course was unconscionable to me. But the turnaround experts were certain they knew better. The company would end up filing for bankruptcy. Twice. More than 10,000 people lost their jobs.*

I've received death threats for my writing before, but none of them rattled me the way one of Dov's clownish goons did over the phone that summer. You go from working for and admiring someone—thinking you believe in the same things—to realizing that you had blinded yourself. You realize that you'd debased yourself. You realize that most of it was a lie. And suddenly you're worried for your safety, going about your business as if your car and your office are bugged.

There was sadness and fear, but there was also a surprising amount of certainty. It felt much better to leave, much better to do the hard thing, than the morally conflicted years—as interesting and at times fun as they were—had. Far more rewarding too.

---

* It was an experience that informed my book *Ego Is the Enemy*.

As American Apparel imploded, I read a lot of Seneca. He is a fascinating figure because for all his beautiful writings about Stoicism—courage and justice especially—he also worked for Nero. Had I been a minor twenty-first-century equivalent? A writer who didn't live by their words? In a sense, yes. Indisputably, I had fallen short. I had compromised. I should have known better. I could have been braver.

I think a big part of it had been the slow boil of it. You start with a set of assumptions made based on the facts as you understand them or even on compromises you're willing to make. Nero was a teenager when Seneca met him. I met Dov when I was a teenager. Things change. You learn more. Events happen. But if you're not willing to make decisions—hard decisions—as you grow and things change, then you're a coward.

Lack of agency is contagious. We used to talk at American Apparel about how we were all "watching the Dov show." No one even *talked* about doing anything about it. It was like we were all passive observers of our own surreal lives—right down to the hours and hours we were forced to sit and watch him rant and rave. Sometimes he was brilliant. Sometimes he was appallingly malevolent. It seems like it never occurred to anyone that *we could do something about this.* Maybe we expected somebody else would, that the adults would save us. As we got older—as Seneca grew powerful in his own right—it conveniently escaped us that *we were the ones who needed to come to the rescue.*

Confidentiality agreements, severances, car leases, friendships . . . compartmentalization, our own daddy issues. He was the boss and his signature was on our checks. You have a personal connection and that blinds you. Nobody we knew called us out. If they had, would we have listened? Or would it just have driven us deeper into the cognitive dissonance? Fear—in its many forms—was a persuasive deterrent. It won out over courage. At least I can say that in my own case.

Seneca himself would talk about how virtue is two parts. The study of truth, followed by conduct. If there is a third part, he said, it would be admonishment and reminders—the process of reviewing, reflecting, and creating rules based on our experiences. Of course, of all the parts, conduct is the most important. My own story is evidence of that. But it is also by failing—and looking in the mirror afterward—that we are able to grow and learn, and hopefully be better next time. That's how it went for Seneca. Eventually, he did break with Nero. He went out like a hero.

By the time 2016 rolled around, I too had learned from my experiences. I had a column in the *New York Observer,* which was owned by Jared Kushner, then known simply as a real estate developer and the son-in-law of a reality show personality. That summer, I wrote a piece that made a strong case against Donald Trump's fitness for office. There had been no need for editorial approval of my writing up until that point, but suddenly the paper blocked the publication of my piece. A few years earlier, I would have been afraid to rock the boat—or lose the money that might come from the gig. Now it didn't even occur to me to *not* publish something I thought was important.

I also knew I wasn't wrong, which meant it was right to say it.

I posted my piece elsewhere and it immediately went viral. I knew it meant my days writing at the *Observer* would be numbered. Shortly afterward, I wrote another critical piece that also focused on the extreme right-wing website Breitbart. Again, it was not published so I put it out on my own. Shortly thereafter, I was informed that someone associated with the campaign had called to make serious allegations that one of my books had been plagiarized. The accusation was preposterous, but that wasn't the point: It was supposed to be a warning. They wanted me to know they would try to ruin me if I didn't shut up.

Didn't work.

If I had lost my column because of the Trump piece? If I had been forced to fight false accusations? If someone had come after me? I'd have handled it the same way I handled losing that salary—with the tools I've always had, as Marcus Aurelius said. To give in to fear is to deny the talents and skills that got you where you are in the first place. It's to deprive yourself of the agency you were given at birth.

In a sense, I am grateful for the experiences at American Apparel, because they taught me—belatedly—about the importance of listening to the voice inside yourself. In the midst of chaos and corruption, it can be hard to hear the call to courage. Sometimes you can only understand the perils of hesitation, of not speaking truth to power, after witnessing what happens to you and others when that doesn't happen.

You'll find the outright intimidation I was just talking about is rare. Far more effective are the ordinary incentives of life. Tell people what they want to hear and you'll have a bigger audience. Don't get political. Refrain from challenging anyone's identity. Any modern writer can look at their unsubscribe and unfollow rates and learn very quickly that to present the harsh truth is often to harm your wallet. You only have to read your fan mail when you wade into controversial topics: *Why did you say that? I'm never reading you again.*

I'm not perfect. I haven't always been as courageous as I wish I was, clearly. But as I have gotten older as a writer, one thing has become increasingly clear to me: Our obligation is to the truth—whether people like it or not. Like Helvidius, they might punish you for it. They might "cancel" you or even literally kill you for it. But as I often tell angry readers, I didn't build my platform to *not* use it to say what I believe.

I saved this story for the close of this book precisely because it's complicated and ordinary. Twelve thousand people worked at American Apparel over the years. Who was the most guilty? No one can say. If you read the stories about those leaked pictures, you'll see how murky the situation actually was. Maybe you'll read my Trump column and think I was totally wrong and it shouldn't have been published.

My point in those stories was to show that courage is something we all have to work toward in our own way, in our own lives—most of which are quite pedestrian. Samuel Johnson joked that "every man thinks meanly of himself for not having been a soldier." I get that. I wrestled with that even as I wrote this book: Am I qualified? Am I *allowed* to write about courage having never saved anyone's life outside of some 911 calls and giving somebody CPR on the pavement outside a bar?

I haven't always been courageous. I'm not always courageous. I hesitated even to write this chapter and some people told me not to include it . . . but then I remembered that hesitation ought to steel your resolve. I can say earnestly that I am getting better at the timeless challenge of applying courage to real life. I care less of what people think today than I did yesterday. I step forward more often than I slink back. Writing and publishing this book was an example of that. But I'd like my private life and my private actions to speak louder than words.

We have to stop thinking of courage only as what happens on the battlefield or on a bus during the Freedom Rides. It's also just not being afraid of your boss . . . or the truth. It's the decision to follow your own creative path. It's drawing an ethical line. It's being a weirdo if that's who you are. It's voting your conscience, not what the crowd wants. Or what your parents want.

It's not only doing these things when destiny calls you onto the world's stage. It's also, as we've talked about, making courage a habit. Something you do in matters big and small, day in and day out—so that it feels as natural in every moment, no matter who is watching, no matter the stakes.

Courage calls to each of us.

Will we answer?

Or maybe that's too much. Can we *get better* at answering? Can we step up more times than we step back?

Let's start there.

Ryan Holiday
The Painted Porch Bookshop
Bastrop, Texas
2021

What to Read Next?

~

For most people, bibliographies are boring. For those who love to read, it's the best part. In the case of this book, which relied on so many wonderful authors and thinkers, I could not possibly fit the entire bibliography in the book. Instead, I've prepared a full list not only of all the great books that influenced the ideas you've just read, but also what I got out of them and why you might like to read them. To get this list, please just email **books@courageiscalling.com** or go to **courageiscalling.com/books**. I'll also send you a list of some great quotes about courage.

CAN I GET EVEN MORE BOOK RECOMMENDATIONS?

YES. You can also sign up for my list of monthly book recommendations (now in its second decade). The list has grown to include more than two hundred thousand people from all over the world and has recommended thousands of life-changing books. **ryanholiday.net/reading-newsletter**. I'll start you off with ten awesome books I know you'll love.

Acknowledgments

~

This was a book written during the depths of the COVID-19 pandemic, and by definition would not be possible were it not for the brave doctors, scientists, frontline workers, delivery drivers, and grocery store employees who showed up each day—each doing their own little part so that the rest of us could survive. When I talk about courage, I am not just talking about soldiers, but about *anyone* who perseveres in the face of fear, of difficulty, or doubt. We all owe a debt of gratitude to the heroes of 2020 and 2021—and should use the events of the last year to take stock of ourselves and our own contributions to the common good.

I also would like to thank my wife, Samantha, who tirelessly supported and protected our family while I wrote this book. I also owe my in-laws, who let me park an RV in their driveway over the summer and watched our kids as I wrote Part 2 of the book. I'd like to thank my researchers Billy Oppenheimer and Hristo Vassilev, my editor Nils Parker, my agent Stephen Hanselman, and the team at Portfolio (Adrian Zackheim, Niki Papadopoulos, Stefanie Brody, Tara Gilbride, Megan McCormack). Thank you to General Mattis, General Lasica, Bradley Snyder, Matthew McConaughey, my tireless mentor Robert Greene, and Steven Pressfield for their advice and notes. Thanks to my old team at American Apparel for their help on the afterword and for sticking with me, even if I wasn't always as brave as I could have been.

Again, this book—indeed all art, literature, and technology—would not be possible without the sacrifices and bravery of generations past. We can never repay them for these efforts. All we can do is try to follow in their footsteps and honor them by using their inspiration for deeds of our own. To whatever degree I succeed at that here or elsewhere, I nevertheless remain gratefully in great debt.

Also by Ryan Holiday

Also by Ryan Holiday and Stephen Hanselman

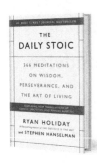  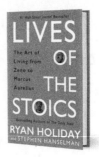

RyanHoliday.net
DailyStoic.com

PORTFOLIO
PENGUIN

Interested in learning
even more about Stoicism?

Visit

DailyStoic.com/email

to sign up for a daily email,
engage in discussion, get advice,
and more.